HUMAN SKILLS

The Power to Connect with Anyone
& Navigate Workplace Differences

ELIZABETH
NYAMAYARO

PROSE

1632 1st Ave #20850
New York, NY 10028

Copyright © 2025 by Elizabeth Nyamayaro

All rights reserved, including the right to reproduce this book or portions thereof in any form whatsoever. For information, address: PROSE 1632 1st Ave #20850, New York, NY 10028

First PROSE edition published 2025

No part of this book may be used or reproduced in any manner whatsoever without the prior written permission of the publisher, except in the case of brief quotations embodied in reviews.

For information about special discounts for bulk purchases, please contact PROSE sales at: sales@proseNYC.com

Live events: To book Elizabeth Nyamayaro for an event, contact the Harry Walker Agency Inc. at 1-646-227-4900 or visit the website: www.harrywalker.com/speakers/elizabeth-nyamayaro

While all the stories in this book are true, some names and identifying details have been changed to protect the privacy of the people involved.

Cover & Interior design by: BEHINDtheCAUSE

Manufactured in the United States of America

Library of Congress Control Number: 2024923418

ISBN: 979-8-9915988-1-1
ISBN: 979-8-9915988-7-3 (ebook)

For my father, Michael, who taught me the value of connection and understanding others.

CONTENTS

	INTRODUCTION	1
PART I:	**THE FUNDAMENTALS OF HUMAN SKILLS**	
1.	THE POWER OF HUMAN SKILLS	17
2.	UNDERSTANDING OURSELVES AND OTHERS	37
3.	HOW TO CONNECT AND COLLABORATE	57
PART II:	**HUMAN SKILLS FOR PERSONAL DEVELOPMENT**	
4.	HOW TO BUILD TRUST	79
5.	HOW TO SET BOUNDARIES	97
6.	HOW TO SPEAK UP	117
PART III:	**HUMAN SKILLS FOR MASTERING WORKPLACE DIFFERENCES**	
7.	HOW TO TALK ABOUT RACE	131
8.	HOW TO BRIDGE THE GENERATIONAL GAP	143
9.	HOW TO ADDRESS TOKENISM	157
10.	HOW TO BE AN ALLY	175
11.	HOW TO SUSTAIN AND GROW HUMAN SKILLS	193
	ACKNOWLEDGMENTS	199
	RECOMMENDED READING	201
	NOTES	203

INTRODUCTION

When I share my story, people often express their astonishment upon learning that I grew up in a small village in Africa. I can feel their surprise as they grapple with the notion that a girl from such humble beginnings could make her way to New York City as a senior advisor at the United Nations. They frequently ask, "How did you navigate such tremendous odds to fulfill your dreams?" Some marvel, "You must have been incredibly lucky to achieve what you have." A few even suggest, "You must have a God who really loves you." While I am profoundly grateful for my life and the incredible opportunities I've experienced—including the privilege of working for the United Nations, which saved me from starvation during a devastating drought at the age of eight—luck has played a secondary role in my life. The real foundation of my achievements lies in the values imparted to me by my loving African community, who shared the timeless wisdom of our ancestors. They taught me about the immense power inherent in our shared humanity—a power that resides in each of us. With this book, I aim to pass on this timeless wisdom to you and inspire you to achieve greater fulfillment in your life.

This simple yet life-changing philosophy, paired with vital human skills, has profoundly transformed my life. It has enabled me to connect effortlessly with others and confidentially navigate differences while living across three continents and venturing to every corner of the globe. Whether wandering through the bustling streets of New York, soaking in the magical lights of Paris, traversing the vast deserts of Kuwait, or discovering the breathtaking landscapes of Mongolia, these skills have allowed me to break down cultural, racial, and linguistic barriers, fostering deep relationships that have greatly enriched my journey.

Professionally, human skills have facilitated my extraordinary 20+ year career, propelling me from a village girl to a global leader at the United Nations, where I have championed transformative global initiatives that have improved the lives of millions. From collaborating with Fortune 500 CEOs and participating in the World Economic Forum in Davos to leading diplomatic negotiations with global leaders at the UN General Assembly, and from fostering trust with rural farmers in Honduras to uniting community leaders in Egypt, the ability to connect on a human level has been pivotal to my success, enabling me to thrive in complex situations at the highest levels. These experiences have demonstrated to me that to succeed in life, we must first succeed in understanding people. On a personal level, these very skills have nurtured profound friendships and sustained a loving marriage for seventeen years and counting. Ultimately, I've learned that meaningful human connections are not only key to achieving success but are also essential for finding greater fulfillment in our modern lives—something many of us genuinely desire.

For far too long, society has perpetuated the illusion that money and success are synonymous with happiness, leading us to assume that accumulating wealth will inevitably bring us joy and fulfillment. However, even with our jobs, successful careers, and various accolades, many of us find ourselves lacking a genuine sense of fulfillment when we take a moment to introspect. Ironically, as our income rises, so do our desires, often leaving us feeling less satisfied than before. So, if the chase for material wealth doesn't unlock the door to genuine fulfillment, then what truly does?

This book offers profound insights rooted in ancient African wisdom, revealing a pathway to genuine fulfillment in today's world—wisdom that has significantly transformed my life and empowered me to create meaningful change in the world. This timeless wisdom serves as a remedy for the widespread loneliness, disconnection, and dissatisfaction that plague our modern lives. Before we embark on this journey of transformation, let me share the experiences from my childhood that laid the foundation for this profound understanding.

THE ANCIENT WISDOM OF AFRICA

I was eleven years old when my Uncle Sam gifted me my very first book, *I Write What I Like,*—authored by Steve Biko, a courageous freedom fighter against South Africa's Apartheid. One paragraph grabbed my attention: "We believe that in the long run, the special contribution to the world by Africa will be in the field of human relationships. The great powers of the world may have given the world a more industrialized look, but the greatest gift still has to come from Africa, giving the world a more human face."[1] I was intrigued. What did Biko mean? I understood his reference to the industrialized world—something my uncle Sam, an economist who had lived in Germany, explained as the modern developments in Western, wealthier societies. But what could Biko possibly mean by, "Africa's unique ability to provide the world with a more human face"? Though my young mind struggled to fully comprehend these complex ideas, they took root. Little did I realize that these words would resonate deeply within me, evolving into a challenge I would one day feel compelled to address.

Before I learned about Biko or met my Uncle Sam from the city, the first ten years of my life unfolded in a small village named Goromonzi in Zimbabwe. This was my home, where I was raised by my grandmother, Gogo, after my teenage mother left to pursue work in the city—an experience that ultimately became a deep blessing. It was here that Gogo imparted the invaluable wisdom of our ancestors, a knowledge that continues to deeply influence my life. In Goromonzi, we thrived within a tightly knit agro-community deeply rooted in the principles of *Ubuntu [oo-boon-too]*—the ancient African wisdom that forms the foundation of our culture. This invaluable knowledge has empowered African communities to flourish resiliently for millennia, guiding us to find courage amidst uncertainty, joy despite adversity, and fulfillment even when faced with life's challenges.

Ubuntu translates to, 'I am because we are,' encapsulating the essence of our humanity in relation to one another. This wisdom acknowledges the undeniable truth that our shared humanity connects us on a fundamental human level, transcending any differences in background, beliefs, or circumstances. *Ubuntu* conveys the idea that a person is a person through other people, emphasizing our connection to one another, which inextricably links us together. This insight acknowledges the quintessential truth that our capacity to achieve great things as human beings lies not in our individual abilities but in the power we share as a collective. This wisdom permeated our culture and identity in Goromonzi, influencing every aspect of our lives. Even our daily *Shona* greeting, "Tiripoka kana makadiyiwo," which translates to, "I am well as long as you are well," encapsulates this sentiment beautifully.

As an agro community, we faced the dual challenge of navigating both personal and work relationships. Together, we farmed, harvested, and tackled communal tasks—whether crafting an efficient system to collectively sell our crops to local markets for funding education or purchasing essential food items that we couldn't grow ourselves. Or uniting to dig a well, relieving the burden on women and girls, including myself, who endured lengthy journeys to the distant rivers to fetch drinking water. Or collaborating to build fences, safeguarding our livestock from the predatory hyenas lurking in nearby forests, recognizing that our success depended on collective effort. Operating within the informal sector, we had to establish our own rules to ensure psychological safety and cultivate trust and respect among community members. *Ubuntu* fundamentally shaped our approach to work and interactions. It defined our shared community culture, instilling in us a common set of values, goals, and practices that enriched our lives together.

Our inability to collaborate or work together effectively meant the difference between life and death. A poor rainy season or unresolved tensions among us compromised our labor force and, in turn, our ability to produce sufficient food necessary for our community's survival. With such high stakes, we focused on nurturing positive relationships, recognizing that if any one of us faced hardship, it would inevitably impact us all. In other words, *as long as one of us was unwell, then none of us would be well*. Even during the toughest times, whether grappling with a drought or facing a disease outbreak threatening our lives, our *Ubuntu* values instilled in us a profound sense of fulfillment rooted in the understanding that we were never alone in our struggles. It was within my village that I discovered the profound significance of human connection and the true meaning of fulfillment. Looking back, I feel privileged to have witnessed firsthand that true fulfillment doesn't stem from material wealth but rather from the nurturing bonds we create with one another. These relationships forge a deep sense of belonging and purpose, which together form the foundation of genuine fulfillment. This is the spirit of humanity and compassion we nurtured within our community.

A decade later, when I relocated to London in my early twenties, I stepped into the modern workplace for the first time, working at an information technology recruitment agency—my inaugural office job. I experienced firsthand the transformative benefits of technology, enjoying a decent salary and healthcare that met my basic needs. No longer did my survival and access to food depend on the whims of an unpredictable rainy season; my circumstances had fundamentally changed for the better.

Despite the advantages that came with my new lifestyle, an unsettling emptiness consumed me. The relentless, high-pressure work environment demanded over 12-hour days, leaving little room for genuine social connections outside the office. However, forming deep relationships with my British colleagues proved to be a challenge. Our exchanges often dwindled to superficial pleasantries, and it became clear that many of my coworkers were primarily focused on their tasks and paychecks, engaging with me only when they needed something work-related. Even in the heart of a bustling, vibrant city like London, where modern conveniences surrounded me, I found the majority of my relationships—both professional and personal—were transactional and lacked meaningful depth. Beneath the cold, grey skies of this sprawling metropolis, I yearned for the belonging, warmth, and strong community ties I had cherished in my quaint village of Goromonzi. It was bewildering to experience such profound disconnection amid a sea of opportunities and interactions. This was merely the beginning of my journey to untangle the complexities of modern fulfillment.

By 2014, I found myself in New York City, serving as United Nations Senior Advisor, where I founded HeForShe—a groundbreaking initiative that quickly transformed into one of the world's largest solidarity movements for gender equality. Grounded on the principles of *Ubuntu*, HeForShe invited individuals of all genders, including men and boys, to actively oppose gender inequality. Initially met with skepticism from some feminists who viewed men as obstacles to progress, the movement embraced our shared humanity and refused to vilify men, ultimately transforming perception. Upon its launch, HeForShe garnered immediate and widespread support, with at least one man from every country joining the cause, sparking an incredible 1.2 billion online discussions in just five days. This incredible achievement illustrates the power of *Ubuntu* in action and highlights our potential to create significant change when we mobilize around its principles.

After mobilizing grassroots efforts, the global movement shifted its focus toward systematic change, engaging Fortune 500 CEOs, university presidents, and heads of state to forge ambitious commitments for measurable policies aimed at eradicating gender discrimination. However, during my visits to several leading corporations across the U.S., a troubling paradox emerged: despite these organizations' significant investment in building inclusive workplaces and their genuine desire for equality, both leaders and employees expressed notable discontent. Candid conversations revealed a widespread frustration rooted in office politics and toxic workplace dynamics. Many voiced a heartfelt yearning for a healthier, less stressful work culture, with some even indicating they would willingly sacrifice higher salaries to escape toxic environments. Others sought greater fulfillment at work, despite having achieved significant success. As an expert in social change, it was perplexing to witness senior leaders at respected Fortune 500 companies—often praised for their diversity and inclusion initiatives—grappling with these challenges. Shouldn't these companies be exemplars of the modern workplace ideal? At the very least, shouldn't their leaders and employees possess adequate internal resources to tackle these issues head-on? I needed answers.

In 2015, I embarked on a global listening tour that spanned over nine years, engaging with business leaders and employees across the United States, Europe, Africa, and Asia. The mission was to deepen my understanding of the challenges many of us face in our modern workplaces. What I discovered in these confidential sessions was striking: a significant root of workplace dissatisfaction lies in our interactions—or lack thereof—with one another. This critical issue is fundamentally about our ability, or sometimes our inability, to communicate effectively and to treat each other with respect and compassion. For example, numerous employees expressed feeling undervalued or overlooked by supervisors who did not recognize their contributions. Others shared their discontent with thoughtless remarks from colleagues, often fueled by ignorance or cultural insensitivity. Some individuals reported feeling "silenced," fearing that their expressions might unintentionally offend others, while others felt judged based on their gender, race, identity, or background.

In today's rapidly transforming workplaces, the intricacies of human interaction have become more pronounced. Factors such as the rise of AI, the prevalence of remote work, and an increasingly diverse workforce have accelerated changes that outdated business systems are struggling to adapt to. Rather than embracing their unique identities, employees often find themselves pressured to conform. Compounding this issue, many leaders and professionals I spoke with lacked the interpersonal skills necessary for navigating the complexities of the modern workplace. This isn't surprising, given that our education system has long prioritized technical skills over critical "soft skills." Consequently, many of us lack training in the fundamental human skills that foster genuine connection and collaboration. Throughout my discussions, it became evident that fostering genuinely inclusive workplaces—where every individual feels valued and respected—demands more than mere policy changes. I realized that a human challenge requires a human solution—highlighting the urgent need for us to focus deeply on developing and enhancing our human skills. This realization about the gap in our human capabilities sparked a deep passion within me to write this book.

WHY I WROTE THIS BOOK

As a humanitarian and an African, I felt a profound obligation to unveil the transformative power of human connection—a force that has significantly changed my life and has the potential to do the same for you. Inspired by Biko's assertion, "The special contribution to the world by Africa will be in the field of human relationships," I'm on a mission to share this vision through my book, *Human Skills: The Power to Connect with Anyone and Navigate Workplace Differences*. This vital guide acts as your "human manual," equipping you with practical skills to foster meaningful relationships and appreciate the rich diversity in our workplaces. These skills are not only easy to learn and implement, but they also deliver immediate and impactful results, providing a powerful pathway toward increased success and fulfillment.

In my decades of experience driving global social change, I have come to realize that the most powerful solutions to our challenges are often strikingly simple. While advocating for policies that promote inclusion in today's workplaces is crucial, we must also understand that these initiatives require time to take root and may not reach their full potential unless we actively foster healthier, more positive relationships among ourselves. Historically, the value of human connection has been overlooked in the business sector, yet recent studies reveal a different truth: success cannot be built solely on technical skills. As discussed earlier in this book, many of the issues we face in modern workplaces are deeply rooted in human interactions—how we communicate, collaborate, and treat one another. Therefore, to attain greater fulfillment in our careers, we must place authentic connections at the forefront by honing our human skills.

The great news is that we each have the ability to drive change and unlock the path to our own well-being. We all have the capacity to nurture essential human skills that foster enriching interactions.

HUMAN SKILLS

Unlike technical skills, which can vary greatly from person to person, the human skills needed for meaningful connections are accessible to everyone and can be honed through consistent practice and authentic curiosity.

This book presents a simple yet groundbreaking idea, arguing that beyond policies, our mastery of human skills and our ability to authentically connect with our colleagues is what will spark the greatest transformation in our modern workplaces. While our workplace's challenges may often feel personal, it's essential to recognize that they are, fundamentally, collective challenges. Our behaviors and actions often contribute to the difficulties within our workplaces, leading to distress for ourselves and others. Rather than viewing our struggles as a "me versus them" scenario, we can start by acknowledging our part in fostering a healthier work environment and committing to being part of the solution. Reapproaching our work environments through the lens of *Ubuntu* highlights that the true strength of a team lies in mutual support. Our resilience is inherently linked to the welfare of our most vulnerable members. Overlooking the challenges faced by our teammates can jeopardize the success of the entire team. By bringing more humanity to our businesses, we can cultivate a collaborative environment where everyone feels recognized and respected. This empowerment enables individuals to perform their best, boosts team productivity, and leads to superior results for all.

As we embrace the future of work—marked by increasing diversity, the integration of AI, and evolving models such as remote work—we must fundamentally rethink how we value relationships in the workplace, making them a priority rather than an afterthought. We must prioritize our humanity toward ourselves and one another, making our environments a little more human. In the following pages, I will outline the strategies we can adopt to achieve this ambitious goal.

WHAT YOU WILL GAIN FROM THE BOOK

This book is your gateway to developing crucial human skills that focus on our shared humanity. It provides valuable insights for anyone looking to enrich their personal and professional lives. In a world where many face challenges in forging meaningful connections, these skills will empower you to connect seamlessly with others, fostering deeper, more fulfilling relationships.

The essential human skills emphasized in this book are also crucial for successfully navigating the challenges of today's workplace. In an environment where many feel overlooked and unsupported in managing diversity, these skills are a lifeline. Whether you are an entry-level staffer or a top executive, mastering these human skills will enable you to forge genuine connections, attract new clients, close lucrative business deals, and enhance your career path. You'll learn how to foster strong relationships with colleagues from different backgrounds, even those with contrasting perspectives. You'll discover techniques to facilitate meaningful and open dialogues, turning difficult conversations into constructive exchanges, including about race. Consider this book as your guide to overcoming everyday workplace hurdles, minimizing stress, and creating the inclusive work environment that you truly deserve.

The insights presented in this book are drawn from my firsthand experience—including my impactful inclusion work with some of the world's top companies, over two decades of pioneering social change as an award-winning humanitarian, and enriched cultural experiences gained from working in communities around the world. Supported by solid data, academic research, and hard-earned lessons, this is not just a "how-to" but also a "how-to-be" book—inviting each of us to recognize the immense value of human connection and to cultivate the vital human skills needed to engage with one another in meaningful, transformative ways.

The book reminds us that, above all else, human connection is vital. By embracing the spirit of *Ubuntu*, we can unlock the potential to revolutionize our workplaces, enrich our communities, and make a meaningful impact in the world. Together, we have the power to build a society that places humanity at the center of everything we do—where we rise above our differences and unite through our shared humanity. The ability to connect with anyone, navigate workplace differences, and attain a deeper sense of personal fulfillment lies within our reach. Through this book, it's my hope that this enduring wisdom will inspire transformative change in your lives, just as they have profoundly impacted mine. The only question that remains is whether you will choose to seize this opportunity.

―――

The book's structure considers the time constraints of your busy work schedule, allowing you to easily navigate to the resources you need immediately. Despite this flexibility, I strongly urge you to read the book cover to cover to truly master the skills it offers. A deep understanding of all its components and their interconnectedness is crucial.

The book is divided into three sections:

- Part I: The Fundamentals of Human Skills
- Part II: Human Skills for Personal Development
- Part III: Human Skills for Mastering Workplace Differences

Part I: The Fundamentals of Human Skills emphasizes the importance of embracing our humanity in driving business success within a diverse workforce and in finding fulfillment in work environments. Chapter 1: The Power of Human Skills discusses humanity in the workplace. It critically examines diversity-and-inclusion initiatives, proposing a revolutionary shift in addressing the challenges. Part I introduces key character traits essential for mastering the human skills described in Chapter 2: Understanding Ourselves and Others and Chapter 3: How to Connect and Collaborate.

Part II: Human Skills for Personal Development focuses on self-empowerment, advocating for ourselves, enhancing professional credibility, and fostering long-term success. You'll find this power in Chapter 4: How to Build Trust, Chapter 5: How to Set Boundaries, and Chapter 6: How to Speak Up. Learn how to be assertive without jeopardizing your career and amplify your voice for greater visibility and success.

Part III: Human Skills for Mastering Workplace Differences provides strategies for understanding others' perspectives, showing empathy, and developing cultural awareness for success in a diverse work environment. Among the human skills covered in this section is conflict resolution. Chapter 7: How to Talk About Race equips you with the essential dos and don'ts for engaging in constructive discussions about race. Chapter 8: How to Bridge the Generational Gap provides invaluable insights for fostering open communication, cultivating mutual respect, and building understanding among your multigenerational peers and team members. Chapter 9: How to Address Tokenism helps you address everyday tokenism in the workplace. In Chapter 10: How to be an Ally, you'll uncover essential strategies to become a proactive and impactful ally to your colleagues.

The book ends with practical strategies for maintaining and mastering your human skills in Chapter 11: How to Sustain and Grow Human Skills. Additionally, it offers valuable resources for ongoing learning and self-improvement under the section Recommended Reading.

PART I

THE FUNDAMENTALS OF HUMAN SKILLS

1

THE POWER OF HUMAN SKILLS

One day, a community gathered in their town square to solve an issue that had been bothering them for some time. A distressed man had set shelter in their square, where he wailed—yelling out and loudly singing all day and all night, disturbing everyone and everything around him. No one knew who the man was or where he had come from. The community had tried to ignore him, but the longer this went on, the louder and more distressed the man became.

"We must stop this raving madman from disturbing the peace," the no-nonsense mayor of the town eventually said, pointing at the distressed man.

Everyone agreed.

"Whoever manages to make the madman stop shall be awarded a prize," the mayor decreed.

And so, one by one, each man from the town approached the distressed man. Some yelled at him, some tried negotiating, and others threatened to beat him up. Still, the man kept wailing. Next, the women intervened. They asked what was wrong with him and offered food and money in exchange for his silence, but none were successful. That evening, unable to sleep from the wailing sounds of the distressed man, a young girl who had attentively watched all the commotion asked the mayor if she could give it a try. Reluctantly, he agreed.

The following morning, the young girl returned to the town square alone. No one from the town even bothered watching her attempt. If we've all failed to stop the madman, surely this young girl has no chance, they reasoned. However, later that day, just before the sun retreated, the "madman" quietened and silence fell upon their town.

When the community rushed to the square, they were surprised to find the distressed man sitting quietly on the ground, no longer singing or yelling. Next to him sat the young girl whose dress was drenched in sweat.

"How did you manage to stop the raving madman?" the mayor asked the girl as he approached her.

She inhaled, still catching her breath. "He is no madman. He's a sad man who is in mourning," she responded, "And so I helped him to grieve the death of his wife."

The women were puzzled, "How do you know about his wife? He never responded or even said a word to any of us?"

The girl's eyes filled with tears. "I guess it depends how you asked … I didn't question him; I just cried with him." She wiped a tumbling tear off her cheek and exhaled. "Then, I sang and danced with him. I didn't know the lyrics or understand his words, but I did my best, humming and clapping as I followed his dance steps."

Now, the townspeople were captivated. "And what happened next? Tell us, tell us!" they demanded.

"After we were both panting for air, I turned to him and said,

'What a lovely dance we have had, sir. Thank you so much for leading us and letting me join you; I really enjoyed it. What do you say we take a break? Let's rest our voices and relax for a while.'"

As she said this, the girl didn't realize how much her words and actions had touched the sad man. He had felt seen, with his loss and pain acknowledged. And because the young girl hadn't judged him, choosing instead to join him, he had felt a sense of connection, building enough trust to open up to the girl about his recently deceased wife.

The tale delves to the very core of our humanity, illuminating our inherent desire to be acknowledged and understood. As told to me by my grandmother, Gogo, the story unfolds with a grieving man unnoticed and disregarded by those around him. Instead of showing compassion, they seek to silence him. Rather than offering solace, they attempt to exclude him from their midst. Their sheer lack of empathy and inability to see the man's plight only intensifies his suffering. By failing to recognize the connection of their shared humanity, they, in turn, increase the suffering of their own. This story echoes the ancient wisdom of *Ubuntu*, which recognizes that what impacts one of us will eventually likely impact all of us in various ways. As the man's anguish deepen, his cries echo through the community, disrupting their peace and compelling them to face the repercussions of their apathy to his pain.

The insightful message in this narrative may resonate profoundly with many of us today. We live in a society increasingly marked by divisions—political, economical, and cultural—that leave many of us yearning for genuine connection, belonging, and acceptance. Similar to the grieving man's experience, these rifts have bred discord and disunity, leaving some of us feeling invisible and disregarded, our struggles and pain overlooked, or even our very presence unwelcome. Adding to this challenge is the relentless pressure of modern work life, where we are pushed to place our careers above everything else while trying to navigate the complexities of a rapidly evolving workplace. With the economy and cost of living escalating, striking a balance between work and personal life feels more elusive than ever, often straining our relationships with loved ones. We find ourselves lacking the essential time to nurture these vital connections, which are crucial for our happiness and well-being. It's no wonder that many of us feel exhausted, that mental health issues are at an all-time high, and that most of us are struggling to find true fulfillment in our modern lives. So, what can we do now?

This book presents a transformative vision for reshaping our approach to human connections—both personal and professional—through the profound wisdom of *Ubuntu*. It is my hope that these insights can serve as a powerful catalyst for transformative change in our lives, reminding us that true fulfillment is not found in isolation but emerges from our ability to collaborate with respect and understanding. In today's world, where individual success often takes precedence over collective achievement, the wisdom of *Ubuntu* can lead us toward a more harmonious and enriched life. My decades of experience with diverse communities worldwide have undeniably shown that genuine human connections are the true keys to authentic success and fulfillment, far exceeding any material wealth we may seek. What if, like the young girl in the story, we each made a sincere effort to forge connections and focused on understanding one another? Just think of the positive impact it could have on all of us.

THE SECRET OF HUMAN CONNECTION

Psychologists emphasize the profound human longing for connection and belonging as the most fundamental aspect of human nature. From the moment we enter the world, our need for connection is unmistakable. Unlike other animal infants, we're born entirely dependent on others for our survival. Our early interactions with caregivers, characterized by touch, eye contact, and vocal cues, form the bedrock of our cognitive and emotional growth, influencing our behavior and shaping our worldview. As we mature, we come to recognize that our ability to forge and maintain healthy relationships with others is pivotal to our success. As social beings, we cannot thrive in isolation; we depend on the support and interaction of others to fulfill our needs.

It's within these human connections that we find happiness and fulfillment in our lives. Research conducted across 132 countries revealed that individuals in developing nations, such as those in Africa, Asia, and Latin America, reported higher levels of fulfillment compared to those in wealthier countries like the US.[2] This was attributed to strong community bonds and reliable support from family and friends, which underscores the profound impact of our relationships and connections on all aspects of our lives.

On the other hand, when our fundamental yearning for connection and belonging goes unfulfilled, it can have a profound impact on our physical and mental well-being. This absence can shake our very sense of self, leaving us feeling unloved, rejected, and isolated. In our work environment, the need for human connection is equally paramount; it's what enables us to perform at our highest level and cultivates a genuine sense of belonging. When we neglect to forge meaningful relationships with our coworkers or to genuinely understand them, we create barriers to effective teamwork, stifle productivity, and hinder our own potential to build trust, gain influence, and thrive professionally. Most critically, this disconnection directly impacts our potential for happiness and fulfillment in life.

Reflecting on my professional journey, I recognize that one of the most impactful forces behind my success has been the power of connection. Not just any connection but a deep, authentic bond with others that transcends varied backgrounds, cultures, and differences. A key component to harnessing these powerful human connections is a mutual understanding of our own humanity and seeking for that in others. In the workplace, this means seeking to acknowledge and understand the individual challenges and strengths each person faces, respecting diverse perspectives, and fostering an environment where open dialogue and constructive feedback can thrive. By genuinely valuing our colleagues as human beings, we lay the groundwork for trust and mutual respect—critical elements for any high-performing team or organization. As I progressed in my leadership journey and began to view my colleagues not just as coworkers but as unique individuals with their own stories, experiences, and aspirations, I experienced a profound shift in my own career and in our workplace culture. Rather than competing for recognition, we learned to support one another, understanding that our collective success is intricately linked to the achievements of each individual. This, in turn, fostered a greater sense of security and fulfillment within our team, enhancing our overall workplace environment.

While the road to meaningful connection isn't always easy, it is definitely worth it. In the upcoming chapters, I'll share the essential tools, strategies, and inspiring stories that enabled me to cultivate deeper, more impactful relationships—from trivialities such as securing reservations at exclusive restaurants in France to addressing weighty issues such as achieving equal pay in Iceland and eradicating child marriage in Malawi. You'll learn how to move beyond transactional relationships and create spaces where authenticity, collaboration, and trust can flourish. This is how we begin to unlock the transformative power of connection.

WHAT ARE HUMAN SKILLS?

Human skills are, in short, the key attributes and competencies that enable individuals to thrive in social and professional settings. At first glance, these skills may seem to be rather basic—such as being likable and able to get along with people, or having a good personality. In reality, they encompass much more. Unraveling what truly makes someone "likable" opens up a world of nuance and depth. Ultimately, these skills manifest through the power of effective, precise, and influential communication.

Human skills encompass how we interact with others, both verbally and nonverbally. They enable effective and productive human interaction and connection. When we think of human skills, having a likable personality, good manners, empathy, and striking the right tone come to mind. These skills are essential not only for professional success but also for personal fulfillment. They enable us to navigate through life with ease and find more joy in our everyday interactions. They give us the confidence and charisma to strike up conversations with anyone, form friendships, and even initiate romantic relationships.

Whether it's approaching a person at a bar, asking out someone from the gym, or befriending a new neighbor, human skills empower us to fulfill our social and emotional needs. With strong human skills, we can effortlessly handle challenging situations, such as convincing a difficult customer service representative to understand our perspective and resolve our issues. We can even turn a cranky flight attendant into a friendlier one and muster the confidence to ask for that extra packet of peanuts. These skills also help us navigate through interpersonal challenges, such as resolving marital conflicts or disagreements with our loved ones.

In the workplace, human skills are the ultimate key to unlocking success. These attributes make us stand out as captivating and empathetic individuals, enabling us to forge strong, positive connections with our superiors, colleagues, and clients. This, in turn, paves the way for us to exert influence, attract new clients, and secure lucrative business deals. Proficiency in human skills is also crucial for advocating for ourselves with unwavering confidence, be it negotiating a raise or promotion, establishing healthy work-life boundaries to alleviate stress and burnout, or claiming a rightful place at the decision-making table. These skills not only give us the power to communicate assertively but also help us decipher emotional needs in any scenario and respond rationally, earning the respect and trust of others.

Human skills are profoundly enhanced by the philosophy of *Ubuntu*, which highlights our shared humanity and interconnectedness. While strong interpersonal abilities can exist independently, understanding *Ubuntu's* principles elevates and deepens those abilities by fostering empathy and a genuine connection with others. The essence of *Ubuntu* reminds us of our connection to others on a fundamentally human level. This perspective encourages us to look beyond superficial interactions, allowing us to appreciate the unique needs, perspectives, and stories of others. Adopting this approach nurtures qualities such as empathy, compassion, and true respect, which naturally build trust as individuals feel recognized and valued for who they are. Trust is foundational to forming meaningful relationships, both in personal and professional contexts. By embracing the values of *Ubuntu*, we gain an acute awareness of the emotional and social intricacies that shape human behavior, equipping us to approach complex situations with greater sensitivity and clarity.

THE NEED FOR HUMAN SKILLS

Human skills are essential for fostering connections with others, and their significance in today's demanding workplaces has never been greater. As our jobs increasingly dominate our lives, many individuals are actively seeking community and connection within their professional settings. This inherent longing for belonging is a fundamental aspect of our humanity; we thrive through authentic relationships. With social interactions outside of work rapidly diminishing, more people are looking to their careers as a source of community and purpose. This might manifest as a desire to join mission-driven organizations that contribute positively to society or simply to engage in meaningful work that has a real impact. Furthermore, feeling valued in our work environments is crucial for nurturing the sense of belonging we all deeply yearn for. Recent research from McKinsey reveals that the majority of people—about 70 percent—feel their sense of purpose is defined by work.[3] Developing strong human skills enables us to build meaningful connections with our colleagues, strengthen our sense of purpose, and enhance collaboration. This not only boosts morale but also fosters a positive workplace culture, ultimately leading to both individual and collective success.

On a business level, in the ever-evolving landscape, organizations of all sizes are making substantial investments in fostering diversity within their workforce, recognizing its immense potential in today's competitive landscape. The vision is clear: by assembling teams with diverse backgrounds and perspectives, businesses can unleash a torrent of fresh ideas and unparalleled creativity, leading to groundbreaking innovations and exceptional products and services. This, in turn, translates into a tangible competitive advantage and heightened financial performance. The proof is in the numbers, with consultancy firm McKinsey's findings underscoring that companies with diverse leadership teams consistently outperform their counterparts.[4]

Visualize it as an awe-inspiring Marvel movie where a diverse group of superheroes band together, each contributing their unique strengths to conquer a formidable adversary. Despite their differences, they collaborate seamlessly, valuing and harnessing each other's exceptional abilities. In the realm of workplace diversity, this is the aspiration—an environment where individuals can leverage their distinct skills, talents, and perspectives to overcome shared challenges and achieve unparalleled success.

Yet despite the clear benefits and compelling business case for diversity and inclusion, these efforts have also ignited a new dynamic in the workplace. With an increasing variety of voices shaping office culture, many of us are realizing that embracing our differences is more complex than anticipated. Our lack of experience and understanding of our colleagues' perspectives and backgrounds is leaving us unsure of how to interact with them respectfully. Instead of being a source of strength, our diverse backgrounds, cultures, and identities are often a source of tension, creating daily interactions rife with complexity, frustration, and misunderstandings—and making it clear that many of us lack the essential human skills to bridge these differences.

Given the complex dynamics at play, it defies logic to think that we could bring together individuals from diverse cultural backgrounds, genders, identities, abilities, and languages without equipping them with the essential interpersonal skills for effective collaboration and still expect them to excel. *Harvard Business Review* emphasizes that if differences within diverse teams are not managed well, it can lead to underperformance compared to homogeneous teams. Harvard Business School professor Frances Frei and business author Anne Morriss attribute this to the "common information effect," a phenomenon rooted in our human nature.[5]

As human beings, we naturally tend to focus on shared experiences with others. In group dynamics, this inclination drives us to seek out and endorse mutual knowledge, as it serves to validate our worth and sense of belonging within the group. Consequently, shared knowledge significantly influences the group's ultimate decisions. Diverse teams, on the other hand, possess fewer commonalities and consequently have limited shared information at their disposal for collective decision-making, often leading to suboptimal outcomes.

In contrast, when diverse teams are provided with an environment where they can build trust and create an inclusive space, they can bring their authentic selves to the table, each contributing their unique perspectives and experiences. This not only expands the collective knowledge of the team but also positions them with a superior competitive edge to far surpass other groups.

These findings present irrefutable evidence that managing differences is pivotal in maximizing their potential benefits. They show us that differences can be a double-edged sword. While diversity can undoubtedly foster innovation and elevate team performance, it also has the potential to spawn chaos, diminish productivity, and breed discord among team members. This dichotomy is evident across organizations of all sizes. Companies earnestly committed to cultivating inclusive environments are reaping substantial rewards, while those grappling with productivity issues, waning team morale, and high turnover rates are failing to harness the power of diversity.

The failure of diversity initiatives in these latter companies is entirely self-inflicted. Rather than fostering an environment where diversity is celebrated and leveraged as a competitive advantage, leaders are imposing outdated norms on new, diverse voices. This not only undermines the essence of diversity but also fosters discord. Expecting diverse voices to seamlessly integrate into an environment that is not equipped to embrace them is akin to forcing a square peg into a round hole; it's an exercise doomed to fail. In today's world, we should be embracing all shapes—squares, triangles, ovals, diamonds, and countless other polygons. Our traditional one-size-fits-all system is ineffective and will only exacerbate the existing crisis if left unaddressed. Leaders in organizations must recognize that our differences aren't a weakness but a significant source of strength. Embracing diversity is essential for businesses to gain a competitive advantage, and honing human skills is the key to unlocking this potential.

THE GREATEST CHALLENGE OF THE MODERN WORKPLACE

The dynamic shifts in our workplace have ignited tension among employees, coinciding with the mounting pressure on companies of all sizes to rectify inequities within their organizations amid a society that is increasingly polarized and averse to nuanced discussions. This convergence of circumstances, driven by the imperative to swiftly address past injustices by promoting diversity, has left employees at all levels feeling stifled in their evolving, diverse work environments. To effectively confront this challenge, it's essential to trace the roots of this issue. Let's turn back the clock to the very beginning.

In the beginning of the business world, men ruled. They understood their role in society as that of providers. They built factories and offices and placed other men inside of them, creating systems and structures to govern them. The rules were simple more power meant more success, which meant more money, which meant more happiness. So men toiled and labored, with only a few ever reaching the top.

Still, being at the bottom was better than being on the outside because a man without a job was a man without status. A man without status was a highly undesirable man, deemed a societal failure. Therefore, the majority took what jobs they could find, even if it meant working under inhumane conditions, being treated as dispensable, or being torn away from their family for weeks and months, or even eons. Again, the rules were simple: men must provide and persist; they must be strong, stoic, and never show their emotions; they must internalize their daily struggles, and never speak of what they endure.

Then, one day, everything changed. Women—and other genders, and other races, and other sexualities and ages and abilities—entered the workplace. They wanted to talk about emotions and how certain things in the workplace made them "feel"—something that "men" had been taught to suppress. They demanded a seat at the table, and equal pay for equal work, and more inclusive language, and for their unique perspectives to be respected. They asked for gender-neutral bathrooms.

Men looked around and said, "Wait a minute, this is all so different and happening too fast."

And everyone shouted, "Shut up and sit down; this is now our turn." And those men were "silenced." And because those in power became silenced, everyone quickly found that they, too, had become silenced, which meant that everyone was silent.

That is how we got here. Due to the fear of potential repercussions such as being canceled or losing their jobs, and in an effort to uphold the company's reputation, numerous employees are refraining from voicing their discontent with the status quo. This has given rise to what I conceptualize as a silence culture phenomenon. The silencing of voices in the workplace has meant that men, who continue to hold most leadership positions, aren't allowed to express their views on diversity, equity, and inclusion efforts. While the intention may be to expedite progress by avoiding prolonged debates on workplace inequalities, this strategy has inadvertently marginalized underrepresented voices and has not effectively driven meaningful change.

Feeling pressured and silenced, some male leaders are pushing back against inclusion targets, claiming that these efforts unfairly assign blame to men for the mistreatment of women and minorities and discriminate against men. On the other hand, silencing has also harmed the marginalized groups it intended to empower, causing them to hesitate to voice their needs and concerns for fear of backlash and reprisal.

The mounting discontent on both sides has given rise to counterproductive myths, stoking tensions among employees and gravely undermining business performance. Our communication channels have crumbled, hindering our ability to genuinely connect, leaving many of us feeling frustrated and disillusioned.

The prevailing sentiment among our diverse colleagues is one of betrayal. They feel that the promise that their voices and perspectives would be respected has been broken. At the same time, many male managers and White colleagues feel unfairly targeted as "the problem" and constantly reminded to check their privilege. In this new diverse landscape, some want to be allies but fear backlash for inadvertently making a misstep. This complex dynamic has become one of the most significant challenges in our workplace. So, what do we do now?

HOW HUMAN SKILLS CAN TRANSFORM WORKPLACES

It's time to break the silence and stop villainizing each other. Instead of quietly wishing for things to get better while secretly pointing fingers, we must come together and focus on confronting the true source of much of our discontent: the outdated systems and structures in our workplaces. Originally designed by men from the past for a predominantly male workforce, our workplace systems no longer meet the needs of the diverse workforce of today. Despite the significant evolution in our modern workplaces, we have yet to witness the transformative shift in workplace policies and processes essential to accommodate our current workforce diversity.

For this transformation to happen, both top-down (policy) and bottom-up (activism) efforts must be in sync. Companies need to step up and implement top-down policies that promote inclusive environments. Equally important is the role of each individual in the workforce to drive change from the bottom up. Meaningful transformation goes beyond just creating policies; it calls for active implementation, which falls on all of us. This means we need to upskill ourselves to not only lead this change but also collaborate effectively along the way.

This is where our human skills come in. Every day in our workplaces, we find ourselves surrounded by a vibrant mosaic of humanity. People who differ from us in appearance, beliefs, and behavior. Individuals with their own languages, perspectives, and ambitions. Their life stories are uniquely diverse, challenging us to broaden our horizons. They demand that we respect their distinct identities and celebrate their individuality. These are people who refuse to conform to societal norms and stereotypes. They long to express themselves in their truest form, embracing every facet of their being. They desire to experience all emotions, love openly, be vulnerable, and, most importantly, be authentic. Adapting to this intricate web of human experiences has already proven to be a significant challenge, one that requires mastering essential human skills.

Just as we wouldn't operate a complex machine without the right skills to avoid harm, we shouldn't assume we can effectively engage with people different from us with limited understanding and knowledge. Developing our expertise is crucial in all aspects of life, including interacting with other humans.

The evolving landscape of our workplaces has highlighted the need for greater support and fulfillment in our professional lives. As inclusion policies struggle to keep pace and the demands of the modern workplace continue to intensify, with technology and remote work blurring the boundaries between work and personal life, many of us are seeking deeper satisfaction in our careers but coming up short.

We demand and deserve to flourish in work environments that foster true belonging and genuine care. Our voices must not only be heard but also valued, and our concerns addressed through open, respectful communication. It's absolutely vital that our need to achieve a healthy work-life balance be acknowledged and prioritized. Additionally, with the increasing prevalence of remote work, it's imperative that we address our inherent need for meaningful human connections.

The good news is that we hold the power to transform our workplaces into inclusive environments. We don't need management's approval, endless bureaucracy, big budgets, or special training. The key is our ability to connect as humans, to see the humanity in others, and to develop our interpersonal skills, which will help us relate better to one another. This is something we can start today with immediate impact. All it takes is our active participation.

To achieve our goals and aspirations for a better work environment, it's crucial to acknowledge the profound impact of mutual respect and empathy. If we long for our superiors and colleagues to recognize our humanity and treat us as equals, we must be willing to extend the same courtesy to them. To earn respect for our values and experiences, we must first show respect for theirs. If we seek compassion and kindness, we must first exemplify these qualities. If we desire care and consideration, we must extend the same toward others. It's unrealistic to expect something from others that we're not willing to give in return.

We must realize that creating a supportive and inclusive work environment is a two-way street. If we take our colleagues for granted, we cannot expect gratitude in return. If we treat them with contempt, we cannot expect understanding. If we're unpleasant to work with and fail to show kindness, we cannot expect others to reach out and ensure we don't feel isolated.

It's a fundamental truth that our actions and attitudes toward others shape the atmosphere in which we work. To be part of a welcoming environment, we must be welcoming ourselves. To garner understanding and flexibility from our managers, we must establish trust and integrity through consistent words and actions.

This is what it will take to truly achieve the level of fulfillment and success that has eluded so many of us in our work environment. Drawing from my decades of experience in leading social change, I can assert that while inclusive policies are undeniably vital for transforming our work environments, the true revolution will stem from our individual actions—bringing more humanity to our workplaces.

THE BENEFITS OF HUMAN SKILLS

We now understand from extensive research that in today's modern workplace, technical skills alone are no longer sufficient. Additionally, we must now acquire strong human skills to effectively navigate diversity and work with anyone. According to an article in the International Journal of Academic Research, a study conducted by the Carnegie Mellon Foundation revealed that a remarkable 75 percent of long-term job success is attributed to human skills, while only 25 percent is due to technical knowledge.[6] The research makes it clear that even the most intelligent and technically-skilled individuals will struggle to succeed without essential human skills, while those possessing these skills will thrive. I'm sure some of us have witnessed less technically qualified colleagues outperform us in their careers due to their ability to build strong relationships with their superiors.

Not only that, a report from the World Economic Forum identifies human skills, such as agility, self-awareness, curiosity, empathy, and social influence, as six of the top ten skills deemed of greatest importance for workers in 2025. The report emphasizes how having these human skills can provide a substantial competitive edge, especially in diverse workplaces.[7]

This revelation doesn't come as a surprise, as productivity in the workplace is deeply connected to effective teamwork and our capacity to collaborate successfully with others. What's truly intriguing is that a recent LinkedIn study revealed that 59 percent of hiring managers face difficulties in finding candidates with strong human skills[8]—as these skills are often neglected in both university education and workplace training, which tend to prioritize technical abilities.

As we look to the future of work, it is essential that we innovate and evolve. To truly excel, we must break away from the conventional ways of thinking. I passionately advocate for a human-centered approach in our work environments as the cornerstone of success.

This transformative shift can create workplaces that are not only more harmonious and productive but also foster greater innovation and performance. A human-centered approach in the workplace transcends a mere concept; it symbolizes a firm commitment to prioritizing people in our workspaces. True to its name, it re-centers businesses on the "human" aspect, making people the focal point of our places of work, allowing them to flourish, and fostering inclusive cultures that benefit us all.

On a personal level, this innovative approach encourages us to recognize and embrace our shared humanity, leading to less stressful and more harmonious workplaces. By collectively valuing our humanity, we establish a positive standard for treating one another, enhancing our appreciation for diverse perspectives, unique qualities, and the richness of our differences. When we allow ourselves to be 'more human' in our work environments, we empower each other to acknowledge our shortcomings and transform our mistakes into valuable learning opportunities rather than letting them define who we are.

Embracing our humanity necessitates embodying character traits such as curiosity, adaptability, and empathy. These essential attributes empower us to thrive in our ever-evolving environment and foster productive relationships with our diverse colleagues. By nurturing curiosity, we prioritize inquisitiveness over assumptions, continuously challenge our biases, and maintain an authentic thirst for knowledge and growth. Embracing an adaptable mindset empowers us to approach change with confidence and tackle unforeseen challenges with a can-do attitude. Moreover, cultivating empathy, rooted in our capacity to understand and acknowledge the emotions of others while remaining attuned to our own, is essential for building strong connections and effectively meeting the expectations of our managers, coworkers, and customers in order to achieve professional advancement.

In addition to these characteristics, we must develop human skills such as self-awareness, emotional awareness, social awareness, and excellent communication to help us navigate our differences and drive transformation.

In the upcoming chapters, we will thoroughly examine each of these skills and provide strategies for developing and strengthening them.

2

UNDERSTANDING OURSELVES AND OTHERS

Developing awareness isn't just a skill—it can be a superpower. It acts as our GPS for navigating the complex world of human interaction. When we possess awareness, we can expertly navigate both our inner thoughts and external surroundings, and be fully attuned to our own emotions as well as the reactions of those around us. This heightened awareness allows us to adjust our words and actions in real time, ensuring that we communicate effectively and empathetically. Moreover, honing our awareness also grants us the incredible ability to "read" others, deciphering their unspoken needs and desires through active listening and meaningful observation.

With this core human skill, we become adept at decoding human behavior, which is invaluable in the diverse and dynamic environments in which we find ourselves. Additionally, awareness fuels our curiosity, propelling us to constantly seek knowledge and growth so that we may become the best versions of ourselves.

Lack of awareness, on the other hand, can significantly impede our capacity to connect, comprehend, and empathize with others, ultimately hindering our progress in achieving our goals. This reality became strikingly evident during a conversation with a friend of mine, Mark, who is the chief operating officer of a technology company in San Francisco.

It's a brisk evening in early 2015, and I find myself in the heart of San Francisco. My good friend Mark and I are nestled in a quaint sports bar on the bustling Market Street. The familiar sound of the Beach Boys' "God Only Knows" permeates the air, struggling to be heard over the boisterous conversations and cheers of the mostly casually-dressed male patrons. With a frothy Guinness in one hand and a Shirley Temple in another, Mark leads us to our table.

A year ago, Mark's company faced a sexual harassment case filed by a female staff member. Brought up by a single mother in Boston and being a survivor of domestic violence himself, Mark took swift action by instituting internal training on sexual harassment for his male executive team. However, that's not why we are here. Tonight, Mark has something urgent he needs to discuss, he informs me.

"So, what's really going on?" I ask, savoring the sweetness of the maraschino cherry in my drink.

"Things just aren't working. I feel like I'm in over my head with this whole inclusion initiative." He sweeps a stray dark hair off his forehead and flashes me a cheeky smile. He could replace actor Paul Rudd in a film, and no one would notice.

"Despite our significant investment in achieving gender parity on our leadership team, we're struggling to find qualified female candidates."

"Go on," I inquire.

"Man, where to begin. Female candidates have been super flaky. They apply for a job, you invite them for an interview, and then they don't even bother showing up."

"Tell me about your interview process."

"It's nothing special. As you know, my work schedule is insane, so I can only interview after hours. I usually keep it low-key and meet the candidates at a local bar near my office."

"Did you say you interview people in a bar?" I chuckle, but Mark is serious.

"You know me, I hate all the stuffiness of interview processes. I find that my approach is more relaxed and conducive to getting to know candidates on a personal level. It's not just about qualifications, you know. I want to know that they can integrate seamlessly into our team dynamic and be able to hang out with the rest of the team after work and watch sports. It's our team bonding thing. So, yeah, what's wrong with that?"

"Umm, the problems are infinite, Mark, infinite," I tease. "In all seriousness, I think most women would find it sketchy to be invited to an interview at a bar. I know I would. It just doesn't come across as being professional. Also, I don't believe all guys want to hang out at a sports bar either, so you may even be missing out on other great male candidates because of that. The interview time is also potentially an issue. You should be mindful that most women often have to rush home after work. It's called the double shift because despite having full-time jobs, many women are still predominantly the primary caregivers for their families."

Mark ponders, then gulps his Guinness, painting a white mustache on his thin top lip. After a long pause, he says, "Huh, I never thought of it that way. Thanks for letting me know."

"I'm sure you could have consulted any female colleague in your office, and I'm sure you would have received similar advice," I assert, unwilling to let him off the hook so easily.

Following our discussion, Mark made significant changes to his interviewing process. He ensured that all candidates, regardless of gender, were given the opportunity to meet with him in a professional setting. In just two years, he successfully increased the number of females on his leadership team by an impressive 30 percent, resulting in 40 percent of his leaders being female. This simple yet crucial factor, stemming from a newfound awareness, has proven to be the key factor in helping him achieve his goals.

Mark's story serves as a reminder that even the most intelligent and well-meaning individuals can encounter obstacles in achieving their goals if they neglect to develop their awareness skills. Mark's lack of awareness was evident in his decision to conduct late-night interviews with female candidates at a bar. This oversight showcased a significant blind spot in his understanding, as he failed to recognize the potential discomfort and unequal treatment of this arrangement. Furthermore, his assumption that all candidates, regardless of gender, would enjoy socializing at a sports bar demonstrated a concerning lack of empathy and awareness of diverse needs and perspectives—all of which hindered his professional goals.

In today's diverse workplace, building our fundamental awareness is crucial for understanding our colleagues and forming genuine connections with them. Lack of awareness can lead to oversights that profoundly impact our team, clients, and business without us even realizing it.

In essence, awareness encompasses three vital aspects:

1. Self-awareness
2. Emotional awareness
3. Social awareness

In the simplest terms, self-awareness is *knowing ourselves*, emotional awareness is *understanding our emotions*, and social awareness is *knowing others*. These three skills collectively provide a comprehensive foundation to inform our human interactions.

As the ancient philosopher Sun Tzu wrote in The Art of War: "If you know the enemy and know yourself, you need not fear the result of a hundred battles. If you know yourself but not the enemy, for every victory gained, you will also suffer a defeat. If you know neither the enemy nor yourself, you will succumb in every battle."[9]

To translate the wisdom of Sun Tzu's words to our diverse workplace (and no, we're not talking about waging war or thwarting our enemies), it simply means that if we master our awareness to understand both ourselves and our colleagues, we are equipped to ensure any interaction is successful. Yet, if we only understand ourselves but not our colleagues, we will likely experience setbacks despite otherwise positive interactions. However, if we don't know either our colleagues or ourselves, every interaction will likely continue to be difficult.

Now, let's take a closer look at these three levels of awareness.

SELF-AWARENESS

In our relentless pursuit to understand and connect with others, we often overlook the most crucial relationship of all—the one with ourselves. It's impossible to cultivate healthy connections with others if we don't first establish a positive relationship with ourselves. Before we can truly master our human skills, it's essential to gain deep self-awareness. Self-awareness entails comprehending our personality, values, and beliefs, empowering us to recognize our strengths and weaknesses. This enables us to sift through vast amounts of information, discern what truly matters, decide when to act, and how to do so purposefully without giving in to external pressures. Individuals with strong self-awareness not only thrive in diverse environments but also excel in effectively managing their behaviors and adapting to new situations.

Self-awareness is crucial not just for comprehending ourselves, but also for tuning in to how others perceive us. This helps bridge the gap between our perception of our behavior and how it's perceived by others. Most of us have encountered colleagues who, despite possessing great skills, intelligence, and experience, lack self-awareness. Whether it's not listening, talking over others in team meetings, speaking loudly in an open-plan office, gossiping about coworkers, making impulsive decisions, playing the victim, getting easily upset, avoiding accountability, etc., their disruptive behavior can lead to increased stress, decreased motivation, higher turnover, and reduced productivity within the team.

In our everyday lives, a lack of self-awareness can cause us to act in ways that may paint us in a negative light, leading to regrets later on. Consider this true story of an Englishman named Douglas Adams.

———

One day, Douglas went to the railway station and arrived twenty minutes early for his train. While waiting, he bought a newspaper, coffee, and a packet of cookies. After placing his purchases on a table and sitting down, he noticed an impeccably-dressed businessman sitting across from him in a suit and tie. The stranger sat in silence.

What a dignified gentleman, Douglas thought as he admired the man's expensive clothing and briefcase. Before he could finish his thoughts, the businessman did something shocking. He reached across the table, picked up Douglas's packet of cookies, and opened it. The man then took a cookie and quickly ate it, without asking Douglas for permission or uttering a word.

This brazen act left Douglas fuming with indignation. *What kind of man steals another man's food right in front of him?* he thought, shooting the man a look of disdain. His annoyance did nothing to deter the man. When Douglas went for a cookie, the man took a second.

Seething with anger, Douglas was dumbfounded, unable to find words. As a British man, he considered this behavior to be uncivilized. The two went back and forth—each taking a cookie and devouring it—until the packet lay empty. Douglas's frustration grew until the tension could be cut with a knife.

Without a word, the businessman stood up, shot Douglas a quick smile, and walked away. *How rude*, Douglas thought. *How incredibly rude.* He hurriedly finished his coffee and began to collect his things, quickly picking up his newspaper. To his surprise and dismay, there underneath the newspaper was a packet of cookies—his packet of cookies.

―――

Douglas Adams, the author of the famous book *The Hitchhiker's Guide to the Galaxy*, shared this story during an interview on the a late night talk show, expressing his deep embarrassment for his behavior.[10] On that day, Adams made many unfounded assumptions due to a lack of self-awareness in that moment. Having failed to keep track of his own cookies, Adams assumed that some were his when they weren't. He assumed the businessman was stealing from him, but he wasn't. It never crossed his mind that the man sitting across from him in a finely-cut suit could afford his own packet of cookies. Like many of us do all the time, he just assumed that he was in the right. Rather than challenge his initial perception, he jumped to conclusions, judged the man, tried to intimidate him, and unintentionally came across as an entitled jerk. His lack of self-awareness had blinded him.

Luckily for Adams, the only fallout he experienced was a deep sense of shame. Yet, in a diverse work setting, even seemingly harmless actions, such as accidentally eating a colleague's cookies, can lead to strained relationships. Operating without full self-awareness puts us at risk of unintentionally causing offense, painting ourselves in a negative light, and, ultimately, undermining our work relationships.

Interestingly, despite widespread belief that most of us have a high level of self-awareness, research by *Harvard Business Review* reveals that a mere 10 to 15 percent of individuals truly possess this trait.[11] This deficit in self-awareness may be a significant factor contributing to the escalating tensions in today's workplaces.

In a diverse work environment, having self-awareness enables us to better recognize our biases, show empathy, identify our blind spots, and manage our emotions.

Building Self-Awareness

How well do you know yourself? Individuals who possess high levels of self-awareness tend to excel in the following aspects. If you find yourself scoring lower, don't be discouraged. Pinpoint specific areas for enhancement and concentrate on mastering one at a time. This approach will make the journey less daunting and more inspiring as you make headway. Consider how you would respond to the following statements:

- I possess a clear understanding of my strengths and limitations.
- I'm always driven by clear intent in all my actions and interactions.
- I'm acutely aware of my impression on others, and I take deliberate steps to ensure it's positive and impactful.
- I'm adept at managing my behavior during everyday interactions.
- I remain composed and act rationally during disagreements.
- I'm skilled in resolving conflicts.

EMOTIONAL AWARENESS

We've all been there. One minute, we're calmly conversing with a colleague about work when, suddenly, something they say hits a nerve, triggering an outburst. Despite our best efforts to remain calm and professional, we find ourselves raising our voices, catching both our colleague and ourselves off guard—behaving in a manner that damages our hard-earned respect and credibility. Sure, our colleague's words may have been unkind, but did they truly justify our over-the-top reaction? So, what happened? It's simple, more often than not: our emotions got the best of us.

Throughout the history of the workplace, we've been taught that emotions have no place in the business world. We've been encouraged to conceal our emotions in professional settings, as displaying them was seen as a sign of weakness, irrationality, and unprofessionalism. In the cutthroat environment of business, where only the toughest individuals succeed, an unwritten rule was established: check your emotions at the door, or face the consequences. As a result, many, especially men, suppressed their emotions, keeping them buried deep inside. Others convinced themselves that emotions were a hinderance, an obstacle to clear thinking, and, ultimately, damaging to business productivity and success. The topic of emotions in the workplace was simply off-limits, and this silent agreement allowed us to carry on with business as usual. Or so we thought.

But then, one day, Tom got "angry" and yelled at his team for no apparent reason. And Suzie felt "sad" and locked herself in the bathroom for a good cry. And Jerry got so "anxious" that he froze-up during the big presentation, unable to utter a word. And Ava, "disgusted" by Tom's behavior, stormed out of the meeting, which made everyone "upset." And as things got tense, words were spoken, and feelings were hurt. But still, nobody spoke about emotions.

Yet, emotions have always been an intrinsic part of being human, distinguishing us from cold, lifeless machines and robots. This is an unchangeable part of our humanity that enables us to experience deep feelings, form connections with others, and cultivate kindness, forgiveness, and love. Disregarding or suppressing our emotions does not cause them to vanish; instead, it simply reduces our ability to manage them. Negating the legitimacy of our emotions is not only unproductive but also fundamentally detrimental to our well-being, as it can hinder our capacity to make sound decisions and collaborate effectively with others.

In his book *Supercommunicators: How to Unlock the Secret Language of Connection*, author Charles Duhigg emphasizes the influence of emotions, stating, "Every discussion is influenced by emotions, no matter how rational the topic at hand."[12]

Whether we like it or not, just as Charles Duhigg suggests, emotions influence every human interaction—including in the workplace. Hence, this book isn't advocating that we introduce emotions into the workplace. It can't do that because, in reality, the emotions are already present. Rather it proposes a powerful shift in our perception of emotions—recognizing that they not only exist in the workplace but can also be harnessed as a tremendous strength through cultivating our emotional awareness. Embracing this paradigm shift will enable us to thrive at work and create a more inclusive environment that benefits everyone.

We must consider our emotions as a versatile tool, much like a Swiss army knife. By developing our emotional awareness, we can gain control over our emotions and put them to use as internal signals to inform our decisions and interactions with other people.

Recognizing and understanding emotions is a crucial skill that enables us to show empathy, a key factor in both personal and professional accomplishments. Empathy relies on our ability to perceive and reciprocate emotions because for empathy to occur, we need to first recognize that an emotion is present or that an emotion is anticipated from us.

This awareness enables others to feel understood and encourages them to reciprocate in times of need. In the workplace, empathy is essential for effective decision-making and fostering successful relationships with superiors, colleagues, and clients. Imagine the benefits of postponing a salary negotiation after sensing that your boss is having a tough day or being able to respond appropriately to a colleague's emotions before they escalate, or recognizing a client's distress and providing a solution that could lead to a successful business deal.

Empathy also plays a crucial role in fostering a positive work environment. By showing understanding and compassion toward our colleagues' struggles, we can significantly impact our own circumstances. For example, when a colleague is having a tough day, their mood can influence the entire team. By providing support, we can uplift their spirits and foster a more positive team atmosphere, leading to increased productivity. Acknowledging challenges, even if we can't offer immediate assistance, helps us avoid taking frustrations personally. Furthermore, practicing empathy enables us to share in the joys and achievements of our teams, strengthening connections and building trust.

In order to enhance our emotional awareness, it's crucial to start by recognizing and understanding our emotions as they arise. Despite sounding straightforward, only 36 percent of individuals are able to accurately identify their emotions in real time, as noted by Travis Bradbury and Jean Greaves in their book, *Emotional Intelligence 2.0*.[13] This highlights the widespread need for us to cultivate these abilities. Whether it's anger, sadness, shame, despair, or anxiety, numerous emotions lurk below, ready to surface. As we acknowledge them, we should refrain from judging or labeling our emotions as positive or negative. Instead, we should view them as valuable indicators of our inner experiences, guiding us toward the most appropriate course of action.

Even those emotions typically viewed as negative can prove beneficial in navigating various situations. We can't be expected to only feel positive emotions at all times. This idea is fundamentally flawed, overlooking an essential aspect of emotional maturity. Allowing ourselves to experience difficult emotions at times is not only acceptable, but essential for personal growth and self-awareness. For instance, embracing sadness can enhance our resilience in the face of failure, enabling us to analyze our missteps and prevent similar pitfalls in the future. This may even guide us toward greater empathy and deeper connections with others by recognizing their struggles.

Nervousness before a presentation can spark motivation and laser-sharp focus, ensuring that we're well-prepared for the big moment. Even anger can be harnessed positively as a catalyst to address injustices, such as unfair workplace policies or abusive treatment from a boss. It's important to remember that all our emotions matter. To be human is to experience all of them without judgment. Once we recognize them, we can learn productive ways to work with them.

Mastering our emotions is akin to unlocking a superpower, necessitating a journey similar to that of our beloved superheroes. Just as they first had to acknowledge and then learn how to regulate their superpower before using it to accomplish extraordinary feats, we have to learn how to harness our emotions to make them work for us. When we command them, they become the hidden power that drives us to professional success by enabling us to swiftly comprehend others, be more convincing by demonstrating empathy, and exert more influence by forging deeper connections. They enable us to convey an image of composure under pressure, dependability, and strength. If left unchecked, our emotions can transform into unmanageable forces, leading to irrational reactions and being perceived as overly emotional —potentially creating chaos in our lives and for those around us.

To illustrate this point, imagine this scenario during a work meeting. Your colleague makes a passive-aggressive comment that feels like a direct insult to you. No one else seems to notice, and it's like a simmering fire inside you. You could confront them right then and there, giving them a piece of your mind, or you could hold it in and plot your revenge for the next meeting. What if there's a different approach? When we take the time to acknowledge and process our emotions, we empower ourselves to make rational decisions. In doing so, you may come to realize that the negative comment wasn't actually directed at you but rather stemmed from your colleague's sense of insecurity. Instead of reacting defensively, you could choose to respond with understanding and empathy, fostering harmony, reducing stress, and increasing productivity in the workplace.

Having strong emotional awareness enables us to maintain control over our emotions, safeguarding our ability to make sound decisions and collaborate effectively with others. This capability is especially vital in a diverse workspace, where misunderstandings may arise due to our diverse backgrounds and experiences. In such environments, emotional awareness can truly distinguish us and drive us toward success. In fact, research from Harvard Business School[14] reveals that heightened emotional awareness correlates with improved job satisfaction and stronger work relations, emphasizing the significance of embracing emotional awareness as a pivotal leadership skill.

Building Emotional Awareness

Don't forget the adage: "What gets measured gets done." One impactful way to boost our emotional awareness is by consistently *journaling about our daily interactions*. Set aside time to capture significant moments, reflect on your feelings, and assess their impact on your performance and relationships. When negative emotions surface, brainstorm alternative ways to handle similar situations in the future. Challenge yourself with thought-provoking questions, and document your insights. The more introspective you are, the more you'll benefit from this practice. Regular journaling helps you identify behavior patterns, empowering you to replicate or enhance them. Set up regular reviews to monitor your progress, and commit to uncovering new methods for boosting and refining your emotional awareness.

SOCIAL AWARENESS

Are you tired of feeling caught off guard in social situations, constantly finding yourself saying, "I never saw that coming"? Whether it's a friend's unexpected betrayal, a colleague's surprising behavior, or simply feeling like you don't fit in, chances are you need greater social awareness.

Social awareness is the master key to perceiving and deciphering the intentions, emotions, and dynamics in our surroundings. It's the essential human skill that empowers us to pick up on subtle cues, such as gauging our boss's mood before they even say a word or discerning the underlying tone from a customer service representative during a phone call. With heightened social awareness, we gain the ability to foresee and adapt to diverse social scenarios, making it easier for us to navigate even the most complex social interactions.

By mastering social awareness, we unlock the ability to gain profound insight into the motivations behind people's actions and adjust our own behavior and actions accordingly to meet our needs in our interactions with them. Without this crucial human skill, we stumble through life as if wearing a blindfold, unable to comprehend why certain events in our lives unfold the way they do.

In a modern, diverse workplace, social awareness isn't just "nice to have"—it's an absolute necessity. In a world filled with differences, these key human skills are essential for our success. Without them, we will struggle to truly understand and effectively engage with our colleagues. Conversely, possessing social awareness makes it easier to genuinely see and comprehend our coworkers by embracing their values and motivations. This enables us to exercise empathy, respect differences, and build authentic connections. Imagine having the ability to discern the underlying reasons for someone's behavior, such as recognizing that a colleague's lack of involvement in a project may stem from a skills gap. Rather than criticizing them unfairly, this understanding empowers us to respond with empathy, identifying alternative ways for them to showcase their strengths. Similarly, realizing that someone's avoidance of eye contact could be because of their cultural background, not a sign of disrespect or a lack of confidence, helps avoid misunderstandings and potential conflicts.

The other reason why social awareness skills are vital in a diverse workplace is because our perception of the world is heavily influenced by our personal experiences and beliefs. This singular, often limited perception of the world means we also have a limited understanding of our colleagues, leading us to unknowingly make unfounded assumptions about them, usually based on stereotypes and biases. This can have a detrimental impact, damaging relationships and even leading to significant costs for the business. Let me illustrate this with an impactful story that one of my mentors once shared with me—*the tale of the old man and the tea.*

A group of American executives once traveled to Tokyo to negotiate a multi-million-dollar acquisition of a Japanese company, a deal critical to their business's success. None of the executives had ever been to Japan before, and none of them had intimate knowledge of Japanese culture. Still, they were the company's top negotiators and had an incredible track record of handling acquisitions like this, so they felt confident they could make it happen.

The negotiations took place over a week at the Japanese company's headquarters. When the American executives arrived on the first day, they were raring to go. They introduced themselves and jumped right into business, quickly assuming command and dominating the conversation. The Japanese executives exchanged glances with each other and said nothing.

A frail, elderly Japanese man dressed in traditional attire sat in the corner of the room. A warm smile lit his face, illuminating the old man's gentle disposition. As soon as everyone was seated, he approached the negotiation table and methodically placed black, round bowls in front of each executive. Slowly and carefully, he filled each bowl with piping-hot green tea, taking the time to acknowledge each American executive by name despite his imperfect English.

What a sweet old man; if only he could hurry up, most of the American executives thought, slightly agitated by his slow pace. They smiled and nodded but made no attempt to engage with him. They had important business to take care of, and no time to waste.

The following day, the old man served them tea again, thoughtfully pouring each man a cup as he greeted them by name. This time, the old man's greetings went unnoticed. The American executives were so focused on the other important people and their negotiations that they couldn't be bothered to respond. The tea routine continued until the very last day, something the American executives had begun to look forward to despite the snail's pace from the old man. On this morning, as they sat down to sign the acquisition agreement, they were disappointed when tea never arrived. *Where is the bumbling old man? Who takes time off work on such an important day like this? This type of behavior would never be tolerated in America*, the American executives thought.

The door suddenly opened, and an elderly Japanese man elegantly dressed in a designer blue suit and shiny black shoes entered the room. None of the American executives recognized him. The man sat at the head of the table and, in perfect English, said, "For one week, you have come into my home—my business—and none of you have greeted me or treated me with any level of kindness. I have served you tea and greeted you by name each day, yet none of you have treated me with dignity or acknowledged my existence. Now you'll return to your country with nothing, because I will not give my company to people who don't appreciate my culture or treat others with kindness." The older man was the company's founder and had been the most important person in the room all along.

———

Just imagine the disappointment and frustration American executives must have felt when they realized the magnitude of their mistake. It's astounding to think that they missed out on a tremendous opportunity simply because of their lack of social awareness. Their oversight not only lost them business but also caused significant cultural offense by unfairly judging others based on appearance and language skills.

Their story highlights the crucial necessity of social awareness, particularly in diverse work environments. Hence, instead of making hasty judgments, it's crucial to challenge our assumptions before drawing conclusions. By staying curious and encouraging our colleagues to share their perspectives, we can quickly find common ground and leverage their unique insights to enhance team performance.

Understanding our colleagues' diverse backgrounds and cultures is essential for bridging differences. By making an effort to grasp how our coworkers' backgrounds and experiences have influenced their perspectives, communication, and interpretation of information, we gain the social awareness needed to navigate differences with empathy and respect.

This vital human skill is essential, whether for leading teams or being an effective team member. The most influential leaders demonstrate strong social awareness, enabling them to effectively connect with others. Thus, it's evident that in the absence of social awareness, or self-awareness and emotional awareness, thriving and achieving success within diverse environments becomes nearly impossible.

Building Social Awareness

How socially aware are you? Socially aware individuals not only excel in these areas but also actively pursue opportunities to continually challenge their viewpoints.

- Do you make it a habit to ask thought-provoking questions to gain deeper insights into others' lives?
- Do you approach every interaction with an open and accepting mindset?
- Do you show a sincere desire to grasp different perspectives?
- Do you actively seek to understand the unique experiences of your colleagues?
- Do you consistently demonstrate empathy and understanding toward others?
- Do you remain fully engaged and focused during your daily exchanges with others?

Challenge Exercise

In our increasingly divided world, it's all too easy to fall into echo chambers that fuel our beliefs and vilify opposing viewpoints. This insulates us from critical thinking and stunts our capacity to empathize and grow. An impactful strategy to elevate our social consciousness is to intentionally confront our beliefs by actively seeking to listen to opposing views and varying perspectives.

For instance, consider diversifying the media sources you follow. Instead of sticking to one end of the political spectrum, make it a point to expose yourself to different viewpoints. Actively seek out conversations with people who have differing opinions to gain valuable insights into alternative perspectives. In a professional setting, make a conscious effort to connect with a wide range of colleagues to gain a deeper understanding of their viewpoints. Ready for an even bigger challenge? Choose a contentious topic such as politics, reproductive rights, or trans rights. Then, try to acknowledge the validity of the opposing view by identifying three compelling reasons for supporting their stance. On a personal level, reflect on times when a colleague may have wronged you, and strive to identify three plausible reasons for their behavior. You might surprise yourself with the discoveries you make.

3

HOW TO CONNECT AND COLLABORATE

Mastering effective communication is not just a core human skill; it's the lifeline of human connection. Being heard is a fundamental human need, and effective communication is the key to expressing our needs in any relationship. Our ability to communicate, from verbal expressions to nonverbal cues, not only shapes our relationships but also determines our very survival. In times of need, our inability to articulate our requirements can quite literally be a matter of life and death. In both personal and professional realms, mastering the art of communication is fundamental to fostering understanding and cultivating positive interactions. This goes beyond just speaking; it involves actively listening, too. It is critical that our message is not only understood but truly comprehended as intended.

In the business world, everything hinges on effective communication. These skills are highly prized above all else as they enable collaboration and task completion. In fact, communication ranks number one in LinkedIn's global inventory of the most in-demand skills for professionals.[15] Great communication creates strong teams and positive outcomes, while the lack of it can lead to confusion and disaster. Additionally, it helps to prevent conflicts and fosters mutually beneficial relationships with colleagues, superiors, and clients. While mastering communication can be challenging, the process becomes much easier when we have a strong foundation of self-awareness, emotional awareness, and social awareness as defined previously in the book.

Through my work, I have uncovered that in the workplace, effective communication skills serve three crucial intents:

1. Connect
2. Collaborate
3. Resolve conflict

First, they enable us to establish a genuine *connection* with the individuals with whom we interact. Second, they foster a culture of *collaboration* to attain shared objectives. Third, they equip us to adeptly *resolve conflicts* that naturally emerge from these interactions.

It's often overlooked that every communication carries an *intent*, leading to miscommunications and misunderstandings. By defining our intent from the start, we significantly enhance the probability of successful communication. Moreover, this approach aids in minimizing the disparity between our *intent* and its *impact*. Intent embodies the motive or purpose behind our words and actions, while impact refers to how these are perceived by others. Recognizing that each person's perception is shaped by their distinct background and experiences, it's clear that misinterpretations are common. This challenge becomes even more significant in a diverse workplace, where our intended message is at a higher risk of being lost in translation. For instance, a seemingly innocent compliment on a colleague's outfit could unintentionally come across as sexist. Offering unsolicited advice might be taken as intrusive or judgmental. Even a well-intentioned effort to improve workplace efficiency, if not well communicated, can inadvertently cause delays and result in negative reactions from colleagues.

Therefore, keeping the intent of our communication in mind during our interactions can assist us in aligning them with their impact to minimize miscommunications. It's also important to highlight that each level of communication comes with its own set of guidelines and expectations. When we understand our intent before we interact, we can ensure that we effectively articulate our needs and get the most out of our engagements. For instance, when our goal is to connect—such as forging a constructive relationship with a new colleague—we must genuinely show interest in them to pique their interest in us and our message. When aiming to collaborate with a coworker, building trust is essential to ensure mutual support in teamwork. If our intent is to resolve conflict along the way—such as when approaches on how to tackle a project are at odds or personalities clash—we must show empathy by considering the other person's perspective and apologizing when needed rather than showing defensiveness.

Let's delve deeply into the crucial principles for connecting, collaborating, and resolving conflicts. Each section begins with a personal anecdote to illustrate the concept, demonstrating how these skills can be effectively used in our lives. They show how much can be achieved when we possess strong human skills and approach others with an open mind and a genuine desire to understand, rather than passing judgment. I liken this mindset to building our "wealth of knowledge" like a bank account, where every judgmental interaction withdraws from our potential while every learning experience invests in it.

HOW TO CONNECT

It's the summer of 2013, and my husband and I have found ourselves in the idyllic south of France, reveling in a much-needed vacation. We're staying in a small but charming Airbnb apartment in Nice. It's a balmy evening, and, to our dismay, we've inadvertently locked ourselves out of our apartment and have thus far been unable to reach the owner for a spare key. Frustrated and hungry, we look for a place to eat at the seafront. Unfortunately, luck isn't on our side. It's the height of summer, and the restaurant we've chosen is busy with a stylish crowd in evening attire, a sharp contrast to our casual shorts and T-shirts. We clearly stand out as underdressed. Ahead of us, five well-dressed couples are waiting to be seated. As we watch the very serious hostess turn away one couple after another because they are full, my husband leans in and whispers, "Let's go; there is no way they will seat us looking like this if they are turning away genuine French patrons."

At that very moment, in an unexpected twist of fate, the hostess accidentally knocks the menus off her table, scattering them around our feet. While everyone else looks on, I instinctively kneel and help pick up the menus, handing them to her with a quick smile before rejoining my husband back in line. When we finally reach the front of the line, the hostess gives us a table before we can ask for one. Later, as we indulge in a scrumptious dinner of seafood pasta, we can't help but marvel at our stroke of luck. *How did we manage to secure a table when others had been turned away?* we ponder. As we leave, I approach the hostess to thank her and politely ask about our special seating.

Without missing a beat, the hostess responds, "It was simple. Unlike everyone else waiting in line, you noticed me." A hint of sadness appears in her eyes as she continued, "You don't know how dehumanizing it feels to be looked down upon by customers, to be made to feel inferior just because of my job. So, thank you again for helping pick up the menus and not thinking that it was beneath you."

―――

This simple story vividly illustrates the immense impact of small acts of unexpected kindness on others. It demonstrates that making a connection doesn't have to be complex. It can be as effortless as a warm smile for your barista, a cheerful good morning to your local supermarket cashier, or offering your seat on the subway to someone in need. These seemingly small gestures are much more profound than we realize. A simple smile or greeting signifies that you see and acknowledge someone's existence, fulfilling one of our greatest desires as human beings. What's more, these acts cost us nothing but offer immeasurable emotional rewards. Sometimes, they even directly benefit us by meeting our immediate needs. When I spontaneously helped pick up the menus, I did it because it felt right, not to gain favor. What I gained was so much more than a table. I made someone feel seen, which is the greatest gift we can give others.

As Maya Angelou wisely stated, "People will forget what you said, people will forget what you did, but people will never forget how you made them feel."[16] These words highlight the importance of human connection in our interactions. By authentically connecting with others and truly seeing them, we satisfy our fundamental need for human connection. This approach fosters deeper and more meaningful interactions, enabling us to build stronger relationships and make a significant impact.

In the professional realm, honing our capacity to engage with others can result in significant advantages. It makes our interactions more effective, our communication more compelling, and our work relationships more productive. These genuine connections are crucial for building trust and pursuing shared objectives.

Our capacity to truly connect with others hinges on three critical elements:

1. Authenticity
2. Curiosity
3. Active listening

1. Authenticity

Authenticity isn't just a buzzword—it's the key to living a fulfilling and meaningful life. It's about staying true to your own values and goals rather than conforming to the expectations of others. When you're authentic, you're genuine, honest, and responsible for your actions. This means that your values, ideals, and actions are all aligned, and you're willing to accept the consequences of staying true to yourself. That's not all. There are many other advantages to being authentic: it helps you build trust in yourself and appear trustworthy to others. When you stand by your beliefs, you earn respect for your unwavering integrity. This enables you to move forward with confidence and conviction, making meaningful connections easily.

2. Curiosity

To truly connect with someone, it's crucial to show genuine interest in them. Demonstrating interest in others enables them to become interested in you. By respecting their time and showing genuine fondness and interest, you'll be able to leave a positive impression. Human nature drives us to search for common ground with others, so it's important to ask questions and show curiosity about people's unique experiences and stories. Starting off on the right foot involves keeping things simple and professional, steering clear of controversial topics such as politics, religion, and anything explicit. Instead, focus on topics such as their favorite show, book, or hobby, their upbringing, or what fuels their passion. Throughout your interaction, remember to keep your body language positive by smiling and maintaining strong eye contact.

3. Active Listening

To truly connect with others, we must be exceptional listeners. Active listening is more than just hearing words—it's about striving to genuinely comprehend what the other person is conveying and empathizing with the thoughts and feelings behind their words. Actively listening entails focusing and staying present so that the speaker feels respected and their words acknowledged. Exceptional connectors practice active listening without any interruptions or judgments, staying fully engaged to pick up on subtle nonverbal cues such as tone of voice and facial expressions. This is key as people tend to disconnect when they feel their thoughts and feelings are not being given the attention they deserve. Remain fully present and focused during conversations, and keep in mind that when others open up to you, it's a gift that provides an opportunity to not only learn and enhance your social awareness, but also to strengthen your bond with that person.

WAYS TO IMPROVE CONNECTION

Now that we've explored the significance of workplace connection—including the foundational principles required—let's delve into five tactical questions about your core group of colleagues which serve as a launchpad for initiating connections that enhance communication and collaboration. Imagine the remarkable success and fulfillment that could be attained in the workplace if every team member developed strong connections, truly comprehended one another, and strived to bring out the best in each other.

How Do They Prefer to Be Addressed?

This may seem obvious, but it's a crucial thing to know. Instead of assuming or giving someone a nickname, take the time to ask them how they want to be addressed. In a previous job, I worked with a colleague who everyone called Eve. After three months, she informed me that she preferred to be called by her full name, Evelyn, and disliked her name being shortened. I apologized and learned from the experience.

What Are They Good at?

Learn about each colleague's core competencies and expertise in the workplace. What are they the go-to person for? Do they remain calm during a crisis? Do they have great problem-solving skills? Are they a great coder or an empathetic listener? Do they have interesting hobbies or talents outside of work that they are comfortable sharing? This knowledge helps you leverage their strengths, as everyone enjoys doing what they're good at. Remember this: by aligning tasks with individual expertise, you set everyone up for success. For instance, if someone isn't a fan of small talk, it wouldn't make sense to have them drum up new business at a crucial networking event. Similarly, if a team member isn't particularly technical, it's essential they are supported by capable colleagues. Focusing on each person's unique talents ensures everyone can shine and effectively represent the team. It also lays the foundation for easier collaboration by identifying complementary skills and strengths that can enhance your teamwork.

How Do They Prefer to Work?

Consider your colleagues' work preferences. Do they lean toward introversion or extroversion? In terms of communication, do they favor face-to-face interaction, written communication (such as emails), messaging, or text? Collaboration-wise, do they thrive in brainstorming sessions, or do they prefer reflecting before contributing? Are they more productive in a serene workspace or in a lively, conversational environment? Having this knowledge will strengthen your connection and help reduce misunderstandings and conflicts. You can quickly gather this information through observation or by asking a straightforward question. It's important to keep in mind that personal preferences can be shaped by generational differences. Baby Boomers typically lean toward face-to-face interactions, whereas Millennials are inclined to opt for email or text communication whenever possible. Nonetheless, it's crucial to recognize that preferences can vary within each generation. The most effective approach is to ask rather than presume.

What Do They Need in a Working Relationship?

What do people value the most in a working relationship? What does a typical relationship with colleagues look like to them on a daily basis? Are they open to having coffee breaks, lunch, or socializing outside of work? What are their boundaries when it comes to talking about their private lives? What are their boundaries when it comes to work? While some of their answers may not be what we want to hear, they help us avoid overstepping boundaries or being imposing, enabling us to build connections based on mutual respect.

How Do They like to Be Rewarded and Celebrated?

It's crucial to understand how our colleagues wish to be recognized and rewarded. As managers and coworkers, we should acknowledge significant achievements. While some may enjoy public accolades, others may prefer private gestures of appreciation. It's important to tailor our recognition to individual preferences, as someone may not enjoy being forced into the spotlight. The same goes for celebrating birthdays at work—don't assume that a surprise party is welcome. Always seek authorization to avoid making someone feel uncomfortable or that their privacy has been invaded.

HOW TO COLLABORATE

It's mid-2015 when I meet with the ambassador of Malawi to the United Nations in his office in New York City. I am here in my capacity as United Nations senior advisor on gender equality for a diplomatic negotiation on an anti-child marriage policy that we urgently need Malawi to enact, given its current alarming rate of child marriage. As I take in the ambassador from across his cherry wood desk—square, dignified face; serious brown eyes and nicely-coiffured, jet-black hair—I'm keenly aware of the significance of child marriage to African culture and don't for a second underestimate the enormity of this ask. Equally, I'm cognizant that long before the visionary leadership of my boss—the head of UN Women who sent me here—other leaders and activists have been campaigning for decades for similar changes without success and to their great frustration. The atmosphere crackles with tension; the stakes are high, but I have thoroughly prepared and am ready for this moment.

As I begin speaking, the ambassador's watchful gaze doesn't falter. With every word and gesture, he scrutinizes me like a hawk, making the situation feel more tense than I had anticipated. It feels as though moving Mount Kilimanjaro would be easier than breaking through to him. However, I maintain a warm and open demeanor. I acknowledge the deep-rooted significance of child marriage in African culture and express my genuine interest in learning more. Despite being African myself, I respectfully acknowledge the diversity within the continent and express my desire to gain insights from a Malawian perspective. I emphasize that my intention is not to pass judgment but rather to seek understanding. I share that the US, despite being one of the world's most influential nations, has yet to pass federal legislation to make child marriage illegal. This creates an unprecedented opportunity for Malawi and the entire African continent to lead the way and inspire other nations to follow suit.

With these words, the ambassador's demeanor relaxes, and a small smile forms on his face. A wave of relief washes over me as having him on our side is crucial to help champion the issue with the president. However, despite the tension between us easing and a firm handshake as we part, I leave his office without any solid commitment.

A few weeks after our meeting, to my surprise, I receive an unexpected email from the office of the president of Malawi confirming his unwavering commitment to eradicate child marriage in his country. In a remarkable show of determination, the president successfully rallies his parliament to pass Malawi's groundbreaking Marriage, Divorce and Family Relations Act on Child Marriage within a mere fifteen months of making this pledge. This landmark legislation makes it illegal to marry a child under the age of eighteen, setting a powerful precedent for the nation and beyond.

When I meet with the ambassador a few weeks later to express my gratitude for his support, I'm eager to understand why he agreed to champion our request with the president. His response is profound: "I deeply appreciate that you didn't judge our culture but made an effort to understand us. Your belief in our ability to lead change on this pressing issue was also inspiring. In a world where our African countries and cultures are often looked down upon, even by some of our own Western-educated individuals, your show of respect, despite any disagreements, means a great deal."

A year later, during a personal meeting with the president of Malawi, my boss and I receive more incredible news. The president informs us that, in addition to implementing the anti-child marriage law, 3,300 child marriages have thus far been annulled by the Malawian communities, allowing the girls to return to school. We're deeply moved and tremendously grateful to have played a small part in bringing about this historic change.

This story serves as a powerful example of how human skills, such as humility and empathy, can pave the way for successful collaborations. My adept use of these human skills proved pivotal during negotiations with the ambassador of Malawi. By honoring his culture and approaching our discussions with empathy and insight, I was able to establish a foundation of trust.

I effectively managed my emotions, remaining composed, warm, and open, even in the face of initial resistance. This created an environment conducive to meaningful dialogue, enabling me to become a better listener in the process. By doing so, I was able to fully appreciate the significance of his cultural values, which helped foster mutual respect and understanding.

Whether interacting with important clients or colleagues, approaching collaborations with an open mind and a genuine willingness to learn makes it easier to influence others, as they feel genuinely heard. Since in-person collaboration is no longer the default, this is particularly crucial for those of us working remotely or in diverse teams or engaging in global markets. It's essential that we treat our diverse colleagues as equal partners, supporting them in ways that align with their specific needs, rather than imposing our own way of doing things.

Effective collaboration, especially in a diverse workplace, can offer significant benefits for both our personal and professional growth. It allows us to tap into a wealth of different skills and ideas from our colleagues, broadening our perspectives, enriching our worldview, and deepening our knowledge. Practically speaking, collaboration enables us to work with others toward common goals through activities such as brainstorming, problem-solving, and developing a shared understanding of processes and projects. By embracing collaboration, we not only share the workload and minimize stress, but we also enhance our ability to drive innovation and efficiency through collective problem-solving. Furthermore, collaboration boosts morale and motivation, paving the way for organizational success as part of a united and motivated team. Research shows that collaboration skills are critical for future success, with approximately 75 percent of employees considering collaboration and teamwork important, and employees now spending about 50 percent more time engaged in collaborative work, according to a study in 2023 by GoRemotely.[17]

Similar to connecting with others, collaborating comes with its own subset of principles, with trust being the most important. Indeed, we can't collaborate if trust is absent. Trust takes time to build, yet it can be shattered in mere seconds. Each project we undertake and deadline we set represents an opportunity to either bolster or undermine trust. In a collaborative setting, establishing and nurturing trust should be a daily commitment, even amidst competing priorities. When trust exists, individuals feel empowered to freely express their thoughts, opinions, and ideas without any fear of criticism or judgment, knowing that their contributions are valued and respected. Moreover, trust fosters a high level of confidence in the team's collective skills and ability to deliver, resulting in streamlined problem-solving and faster iteration. Chapter 4, "How to Build Trust," delves deep into these principles and offers powerful strategies for establishing and reinforcing trust. This will undoubtedly enhance your collaboration efforts.

WAYS TO IMPROVE COLLABORATION

Establishing ground rules is crucial for ensuring that everyone is on the same page when working together. These five essential ground rules will significantly enhance your collaborative efforts.

Show Respect

Respect is essential in any collaboration. It's demonstrated in the consideration we show for our colleagues' time, work, and ideas—helping to maintain a harmonious work environment. If we want to show respect for our colleagues' time, we should show up for meetings on time, or preferably early. To show respect for someone's work and ideas, we can acknowledge and credit them for their wins, and actively listen to their recommendations. When we exhibit respect toward others, we expect the same in return, which is essential for successful collaboration. Mutual respect can help ensure fair work distribution, prevent conflicts, and promote team unity. This emphasis on respect should make each team member feel valued and appreciated.

Be Accountable

Nothing undermines collaboration more quickly or thoroughly than a lack of accountability. To be successful in any collaborative effort, we must take ownership of our commitments and outcomes. Remember that teamwork is about each of us being responsible for our behavior, actions, and performance. Failure to complete tasks not only damages our credibility and respect but also undermines our future opportunities—as people prefer to collaborate with those who honor their commitments. Accountability involves reviewing work meticulously, delivering high-quality outputs, and meeting deadlines.

Establish Norms and Expectations

Establishing clear team communication norms and expectations is pivotal for successful collaboration. Empower everyone to communicate through their preferred channels and platforms, while clearly defining availability outside of regular working hours. Setting the tone of email etiquette is also key; for example, ensure messages are clear, concise, and respectful of the recipient's time and attention span.

By establishing these norms, you can minimize confusion, facilitate efficient communication, and strengthen overall team collaboration. Additionally, your personal needs and boundaries can be safeguarded.

Be Transparent and Authentic

Successful collaboration hinges on transparency and authenticity. (You'll note that we also covered authenticity as a component of connection; many of these concepts overlap, since they are critical to multiple areas.) This means sharing relevant information, feedback, and opinions openly, honestly, and respectfully without concealing or distorting anything. It also means staying true to yourself and your values. A lack of transparency and authenticity can lead to distrust and create tension within the collaboration. By being open and genuine, you show your colleagues that you are dependable, honest, and respectful and that you value their input and perspectives.

Give and Receive Feedback Constructively

To foster trust in a collaboration, it's crucial to give and receive feedback constructively. (Recall how we also explored that feedback can help us to become more self-aware.) Constructive feedback must be specific and focused on behavior rather than the individual. Instead of saying, "You're impulsive, and you gossip," consider, "I noticed that you shared complaints about the feature set before the software is ready. Can I recommend that you wait until we get a more feature-ready version before giving feedback so we can protect others' morale and engagement around the product?" Your feedback must be timely, actionable, and delivered respectfully; that means it must *not* be rude, arrogant, or belittling. Similarly, you should receive feedback with an open mind. Embracing constructive feedback demonstrates a commitment to personal and professional growth, and a respect for teamwork.

HOW TO RESOLVE CONFLICT

It's January 19, 2016, and I'm in Davos, Switzerland, at the prestigious World Economic Forum. The snow-capped mountains create a breathtaking yet cold backdrop for intense discussions among world and business leaders. Little do I know, the frosty atmosphere outside my window pales in comparison to what awaits me. A particularly stressful morning takes a dire turn when my boss invites me for coffee. The tension is palpable, and I immediately sense that something is amiss. Just a few days prior, I was interviewed about gender equality regarding the Davos forum. The forum, infamously dubbed the "Boys Club," had faced significant backlash for its failure to boost the representation of women among its delegates. As one of the few female attendees, the journalist Alexandra Stevenson was eager to hear my perspective.

Her article in *The New York Times* has just been published, referring to me as "… one of only two women transforming Davos."[18] As I delve into her piece, a sense of dread washes over me. Like many large organizations, my workplace has a rigid hierarchy, and my boss, a prominent figure, is attending the conference. Despite securing her consent prior to the interview, the article's portrayal of me has brought her significant embarrassment and made her feel undermined. Instantly, I know that taking full responsibility is the only way forward. I offer a heartfelt apology to her and take the initiative to send an email to the entire executive office (her direct reports) expressing my deepest regrets. Although this action helps diffuse the immediate tension, it becomes apparent that it will take time and effort to fully regain her trust.

This story emphasizes the critical importance of integrity and our duty to be accountable and take ownership of our mistakes when the situation demands it. When I read the article, I could have easily become defensive, as we have no control over how journalists choose to portray their news stories. However, because I conducted the interview, I made myself responsible for the outcome and relied on my human skills to objectively analyze the scenario and achieve a positive resolution. These human skills enabled me to empathize with my boss and the unfortunate circumstances that I had put her in, prompting my heartfelt apology. They empowered me to decipher underlying messages, which made it possible, with my boss's approval, to email the executive leadership team and restore her dignity and authority. Taking ownership of a mistake, even if I didn't directly cause it, and swiftly apologizing helped quickly mend trust and strengthen my work relationship with my boss. My human skills also helped me to forgive myself with a reminder that making mistakes is a part of being human.

It's natural for humans to make mistakes, especially in diverse work environment where conflicts can arise due to different communication styles, personalities, and cultures, often further complicated by virtual working and worsened by poor communication. Failing to develop the necessary human skills to address these inevitable challenges is like willingly jumping out of a plane without a parachute. While conflict can sometimes foster growth by challenging our ideas, leaving it unresolved can have severe repercussions on workplace morale, productivity, and company culture. It may result in resignations or legal action against the organization.

Conflict resolution primarily involves managing emotions to respond rationally, defuse tensions, and settle matters amicably. By having great emotional awareness, we can avoid destructive behaviors such as personal attacks and inflammatory remarks, and instead facilitate constructive discussions that promote understanding and minimize emotional reactions. Mastering this skill is vital for preventing disputes from escalating, and for fostering mutual understanding and agreement. Effective conflict resolution can even nurture trust and strengthen relationships if it's characterized by mutual respect and the willingness to compromise.

When we're emotionally aware, we're able to handle disagreements rationally and prevent them from escalating. If a team member underperforms, instead of reacting with anger or criticism, we can calmly listen and empower them to improve. Even when working with individuals we dislike, strong emotional awareness ensures that we don't let personal feelings hinder our judgment and ability to collaborate. These skills are essential for effectively achieving our goals.

WAYS TO IMPROVE CONFLICT RESOLUTION

The way we manage conflict significantly impacts our collaborations, business relationships, and personal reputation. Approaching conflict constructively is essential for maintaining productivity and achieving professional success. By mastering the five essential ground rules listed below, you can strengthen your conflict-resolution skills and thrive in any situation.

Meet Face-to-Face

Avoid using email or other digital platforms to resolve conflicts. Not only are emails and digital communications more permanent and easily sharable, potentially damaging your professional reputation, but they also may lead to impulsive responses that make matters worse. If possible, opt for something more personal, and arrange a face-to-face meeting or a video conference instead. This demonstrates that you understand the impact of your actions and value the other person. Meeting face-to-face also prevents workplace gossip and reassures your colleague of their importance. If a colleague sends a hostile email, redirect the conversation offline. For example, you can state, "I think we can work this out quickly offline. Let's have a coffee to discuss, or I can stop by your office or schedule a video conference if it's easier." This sets a boundary that conflicts are not to be resolved via email.

Don't Make It Personal

Please keep in mind that during a conflict, just like when giving feedback, it's crucial to focus on addressing the issue rather than targeting the person. Just as you expect your colleagues to remain professional, you must be as well. Instead of using language that places blame, express your feelings. For instance, try saying, "I feel disrespected when you do this," instead of, "You always disrespect me." Similarly, you can say, "I don't feel heard," instead of, "You never listen to me." Instead of asserting, "You need to solve this," try asking, "How can we solve this together?" Remember, when conflict arises, it can present an opportunity to enhance teamwork and make your working relationship even stronger. Rather than viewing it as you against your colleague, approach it as a joint effort against the issue.

Apologize and Learn From the Experience

When we realize that our words and actions have harmed or upset others, it's important to approach the situation with empathy and openness. Rather than becoming defensive, you should use this as an opportunity to listen, learn, and grow. By understanding your colleague's perspectives, taking accountability for your actions, and apologizing sincerely, you can resolve any conflicts you might have caused. It's crucial to recognize that unintentional harm is still impactful, and you must work towards understanding and validating your colleague's emotions in order to move forward positively.

One Disagreement Does Not Make an Enemy

Simply having a disagreement with a colleague does not make them your enemy. Even the closest of friends have their disagreements. It's crucial to remember that you can still find common ground on other issues, even when you don't agree on a particular matter. Try to compartmentalize your disagreements, and avoid carrying over conflicts into future interactions as an act of retaliation.

Follow Through on the Plan

In the aftermath of conflict, it's essential to recognize that relationships may not quickly return to normal. People involved often need time to heal. During this period, maintaining a positive attitude and following through with agreements is crucial until the conflict is fully resolved. Avoid reverting to past behavior, as this can irreparably damage trust. Demonstrating genuine remorse and a commitment to rebuilding the relationship is also necessary, regardless of the time it takes. If you're the one who has been wronged, it's important to acknowledge your colleague's efforts to mend the relationship post-conflict. Extending courtesy and understanding in such situations sets a positive precedent for future interactions.

PART II

HUMAN SKILLS FOR PERSONAL DEVELOPMENT

4

HOW TO BUILD TRUST

Trust forms the bedrock of all human relationships and is essential for nurturing strong, meaningful connections and productive collaborations. As we've established, human skills are pivotal in cultivating this trust. However, what many don't realize is that in order to earn the trust of others, we must first begin by learning to fully trust ourselves.

While this might seem like a simple concept, many individuals often grapple with insecurities and self-doubt, which can significantly impact how others perceive them. Constantly second-guessing our own decisions, allowing fear to undermine our abilities, or being overly self-critical can inadvertently portray us as unreliable and scattered, instilling doubt in our colleagues. When we lack the confidence to present our authentic selves at work, it becomes challenging for others to place their trust in the version of ourselves that we project. If we continuously dwell in self-loathing, our colleagues will struggle to recognize positive qualities within us. In essence, if we are unable to trust ourselves, why would anyone else trust us?

HUMAN SKILLS

The following story of my interaction with a business executive named Jules sheds light on common trust challenges in the workplace. It's followed by powerful strategies that will help you build, maintain, and repair broken trust.

"Is the book really about a man chasing a sheep?" she queries, carefully examining the hardcover, which shows a lone sheep staring defiantly at the reader, a black star etched on its side.

"I suppose it is?" I say, as a question.

"Who frickin' writes a book about a sheep anyway?" she puzzles.

"Murakami, frickin' Haruki Murakami," I respond, and we burst out laughing, two complete strangers sharing an inside joke about the author's magical writing.

I don't know this woman. She has a Brooklyn accent and is distinctively pretty with an angular face; coppery red hair tucked under a black baseball cap; pale skin peppered with freckles; warm, brown eyes; and a cute button nose—*roughly five foot six, thirty-five years old, give or take.*

It's August 2017, and we are in a bookstore at Istanbul Airport in Turkey. I'm in transit to Azerbaijan on the Caspian Sea coast, where I've been invited to deliver a keynote address at a global youth conference. A minute prior, we both reached for the last copy of Murakami's novel *A Wild Sheep Chase,* which landed neatly in her hands.

"Tell you what," she smiles pleasantly, "I think the book belongs to both of us, so I'm going to send it to you when I'm done reading."

"That won't be necessary. You won it fair and square," I shrug, "I'm sure I can find a copy in another store." I glance at my watch. My plane is boarding in seven minutes.

"No. I insist," her voice is cheerful as the sun. "I will make sure the book gets to you. Don't worry."

Surely she doesn't think I'm about to hand out my name and address to a stranger, does she? I scan her appearance: a simple pair of black jeans, white trainers, an oversized bright green sweater, and a black backpack. She's smartly dressed alright and seems friendly enough, but then again, so are most murderers on true crime TV shows. How else would they be able to lure their victims? My internal New York BS radar lights up. I search for clues of a hustle, and she quickly reads my mind.

"You won't need to give me any of your personal details—no name, no address, nothing," she states casually.

"How will you get the book to me with no details?" I've got to know.

"Ah, you see. I have special powers that I can't tell you about; otherwise, I will lose them."

Her tone is matter-of-fact, and her calm confidence disturbs me. *Who is she?* I ask myself, but I have no way of knowing. What is this all about anyway—some kind of Brooklyn voodoo?

My mind reels, scanning my memory for everyone I know, but I still can't place her. Have I met her somewhere? Perhaps at a conference? Still, that doesn't explain how she knows my home address, which isn't public.

"We haven't met before, have we?" I inquire.

"No, not at all. But I will get the book to you. Do you trust me?"

Trust her? What an absurd question. We've just met, and besides, I don't even know her name.

I say nothing, and with that, she gives me a beaming smile—then exits the bookstore, disappearing into a sea of people.

Several hours later, I land in Baku, Azerbaijan's capital city. After a much-needed hot shower and a satisfying late lunch of vegetarian rice pilaf in the hotel's restaurant, I stroll over to Baku Boulevard, a sprawling, tree-lined promenade that runs parallel to Baku's seafront with perfectly manicured gardens of exotic foliage: palm trees, cacti, roses, lilies, you name it.

My long flight from New York has taken a toll on me, and I desperately need fresh air and to stretch my legs. It's a perfect spring evening, and by the time I make it to the promenade, it's bustling with activity. Groups of men cheer on one another as they play chess on life-sized boards; lovers stroll hand-in-hand, gazing into each other's eyes; locals and tourists sip colorful drinks and nibble fancy canapés in the many seafront cafés; and charming musicians play guitar beautifully. I take it all in, silently rehearsing my speech on the importance of gender equality, which I'm to deliver the following day in the iconic Heydar Aliyev Center to more than five thousand Scouts from around the world.

I'm lost in my thoughts when a curious thing happens. Right there, sitting alone on the pavement on the promenade, is the woman from the bookstore. Her back is turned to me, but there is no mistaking her red hair and bright green sweater. Her presence rattles me, and my mind zigzags back to our encounter. Is she following me?

When I approach, she looks up sideways without any of her earlier cheerfulness. Her back is hunched, and I notice that she is crying.

"Are you okay?" I ask.

She doesn't respond, and I regret my words. It's evident from her flushed cheeks and red eyes that she's visibly upset.

The sun slowly sets before us, sprinkling gold fairy dust across the sea. Behind us, street musicians are now playing an achingly moving song, which puts me in a contemplative state. How has Green Sweater and I ended up in precisely the same place at the same time twice? (I didn't see her on the plane.) What is she doing in Baku? Most importantly, why is she crying? She is a foreigner like me, and I know I can't just leave her here alone, crying. So, I sit on the pavement next to her, letting the music wash over me as I wait for her to calm down. Finally, after roughly five minutes, she says, "I'm so sorry I'm such a mess."

I hand her a piece of tissue, and she blows her nose, crumbling the soggy tissue in the center of her palm.

"I just got a very upsetting email from a colleague," her voice quivers. "I don't know if I can even talk about it. It's just way too painful." She's crying again—painful, audible sobs. Her body shakes like a leaf, and I place a steadying hand on her shoulder.

"I feel so blindsided and stupid," she says, wiping tears off her cheeks. "I can't believe I ever trusted him. You see, he was supposed to be one of my closest work friends, and now I know it was all fake. I know now that he has been saying all sorts of nasty things behind my back."

More tears race down her wet cheeks as her top lip trembles. "It's beyond painful, you know, and I just feel so betrayed."

I pay serious attention, trying to piece together the fragmented parts of her story as she continues to unravel.

"I'm … I'm … just in disbelief. No, I'm mad!" She punches the air and grits her teeth. "How dare he treat me like that? God, I'm such a gullible idiot to think that I could trust him … to think that he would have my back, just like I have had his all these past three years." She chokes on her words. "You know the worst thing … it's that I had to find out this way."

She digs out her phone at the bottom of her backpack and shoves it in my hand. "Can you believe the frickin' jerks accidentally copied me on their email," her voice rises with anger.

HUMAN SKILLS

There, in black and white, is an email chain between her two male colleagues.

> *From: Colleague A*
> *To: Colleague B*
> *Dude, ping me when the B*tch is out of the office so we can push through the project before she is back. Sick and tired of all her whining. Know she is your friend and all ... sorry but not sorry.*
>
> ---
>
> *From: Colleague B*
> *To: Colleague A*
> *You got it, man. She isn't a friend. Find her super annoying! Just playing the game. Know what they say, keep your friends close and your enemies even closer.*

The communication reveals that the woman's name is Jules. She is the sales director of a tech start-up based in New York that serves the oil industry, and she's in Baku to canvass for new business.

"You know what?" Jules states brokenly. "Maybe on some level, it's good that I found out." She draws a long, sharp breath. "At least now I know who my enemies are. And guess what? I will never, EVER trust them again."

For the following hour or so, we sit in sullen silence, watching as the city lights up and the shadows of surrounding buildings lengthen and disappear before our eyes.

HOW TO BUILD TRUST

A few weeks after my Baku trip, I receive the following letter at my New York apartment:

> My dearest Elizabeth,
>
> I get it now. The book was never about chasing a sheep but about our constant search for meaning and the importance of trusting ourselves. I was profoundly moved and saddened by this, but as is usual with a Murakami book, I'm left with more unanswered questions. Perhaps we could discuss this sometime over a coffee?
>
> With love and admiration,
> Jules
>
> PS 1: I'm a massive fan of your work. My sister and I follow you on social media. She lives in your building.
>
> PS 2: See, I kept my promise.

Inside the envelope with Jules's heartfelt letter is a copy of Haruki Murakami's *A Wild Sheep Chase*.

———

As this story illustrates, navigating the dynamics of our modern work environment is hard enough without the additional stress of building trust with diverse coworkers whose values and beliefs frequently differ from ours. Failing to do so often leaves us suffering in low-trust workplaces, characterized by a lack of transparency or accountability. This can create a "dog-eat-dog" environment fueled by fear, blame, and backstabbing—all of which undermine productivity and overall job satisfaction.

For more than twenty years, global communications company Edelman has been studying trust. Research they conducted in 2022 found that because of the rise in the divisive nature of politics and fake news, distrust is now society's default emotion, impacting our ability to engage in constructive dialogue on the issues we disagree on.[19] Without trust, collaborating with our team is ineffective, and finding common ground with our diverse coworkers is nearly impossible. Without trust, remote teams can't function well. Without trust, our managers are likely to micromanage us, undermining our confidence and self-esteem. Being part of a low-trust workplace often leaves us feeling overly stressed, isolated, or misunderstood, jeopardizing our ability to build relationships for fear of being hurt or betrayed.

The opposite is also true. Research from Harvard Business Review shows that people working at high-trust companies experience 74 percent less stress, 40 percent less burnout, and 29 percent more satisfaction in their lives.[20] When mutual trust exists between us and our colleagues, we can be our true selves and ask for help without worrying about being judged or labeled incompetent. We can engage and communicate healthily and derive more fulfillment from our work. We can confidently set boundaries and better manage our workloads to avoid burnout.

However, building trust isn't easy. That's because trust is fragile. Every interaction we have with others can either strengthen or weaken this invisible bond. One misstep can quickly erase years of goodwill and weaken a relationship. Like when we discover that a colleague we trusted for years is, in fact, two-faced, as was the case in Jules's story. Or when we work hard to over-deliver on a project on the promise of promotion from our trusted boss, which doesn't materialize. Or when a colleague we thought had our back agrees to come through on an assignment only to bail at the last minute. Letting others down (even if it wasn't intentional) or going against our word seriously harms our trustworthiness. Once trust is violated, it's extremely difficult to restore. Sure, we can try and mend it, but things rarely return to how they were. Imagine your dry cleaner accidentally rips your favorite white shirt. While you can obviously get the shirt repaired, chances are it will never be the same again. No matter how skilled the tailor is, you'll always know that the damage is there. Trust works similarly. Even when we apologize and are forgiven for our betrayal, our colleagues are unlikely to forget. Therefore, an essential component of maintaining trust is intentionally building it daily by engaging with our colleagues as truthfully and authentically as possible in every interaction.

Being human means embracing our imperfections. Despite our brilliance, many of us are not fully aware of how we are perceived in terms of trustworthiness. This creates a "trust gap" that needs to be addressed. Harvard Business School professor Frances Frei and business author Anne Morriss have identified three fundamental drivers of trust: authenticity, logic, and empathy.[21] People trust us when they feel they are engaging with our genuine selves (*authenticity*), when they have confidence in our judgment and competence (*logic*), and when they see that we care about them (*empathy*). These three elements of trust are interdependent and must be given equal attention. When trust is compromised, it's often due to a failure in one of these areas, as a deficiency in one undermines our overall perceived trustworthiness.

Just picture these three facets of trust as the sturdy legs of a stool, forming a reliable, unwavering foundation. Just as you wouldn't trust a wobbly stool, people won't fully trust us if we falter in any of these three trust aspects. Much like the stool, our trustworthiness needs a rock-solid base. To establish trust, we must exude trustworthiness, and we can achieve this by honing these three core pillars of trust:

1. Authenticity
2. Logic
3. Empathy

PILLAR 1: AUTHENTICITY

As we briefly touched on in the previous chapter, embracing your authentic self is essential for building trust with your colleagues. However, research from Deloitte shows that 60 percent of US workers hide their true selves at work due to a lack of psychological safety, such as staying closeted in a closed-minded environment or repressing authentic feelings to avoid backlash.[22] How can we promote more authenticity in the workplace despite these challenges?

To build trust with our diverse coworkers, we must be emotionally aware and balance our authenticity with respect for their cultures and identities. Without self-awareness, our actions and words can unintentionally undermine our trustworthiness. For instance, we might pretend to agree with a colleague to avoid conflict, only to come across as deceitful because our body language gives us away. We might pretend not to care to protect our fragile ego, only to be perceived as phony. We might inappropriately get emotional to avoid a difficult conversation, making others see us as manipulative or someone who plays the victim card. Building trust requires authenticity. We can't be genuine if we hide parts of ourselves or deny our emotions. If our colleagues feel they're not getting the real us, they're less likely to trust or open up to us.

The following strategies help you become more authentic.

Tell the Truth

Trust is built on truth. Always be honest, even when it's tough. Speaking the truth fosters trust, strengthens connections, and paves the way for open communication. Our ability to be authentic is tied to trust within our environment, and in order to cultivate high-trust environments, we must be truthful ourselves. Use self-awareness to navigate this process with tact, ensuring your message is well-received while minimizing the potential for offense. Remember, poor communication can erode trust, even in strong relationships.

Own Your Mistakes

Acknowledging our mistakes is crucial for building trust and credibility. Great leaders are not defined by their mistakes but by how they handle and learn from them. Failing to admit our faults is a sign of weakness, not strength. Embracing our mistakes is an opportunity to strengthen trust and credibility in our relationships and work environments.

Learn to Say No

Saying no isn't always negative. It's about prioritizing what truly matters, so we can honor our commitments without feeling overwhelmed. By saying no when appropriate, we empower ourselves to say yes to the right opportunities. Overpromising and underdelivering erodes trust. To build credibility, it's crucial to decline gracefully, calmly providing reasons, even if it may disappoint someone. Keeping a record of commitments enables you to decide what to take on or pass up.

Stay True to Your Values

Our need for acceptance sometimes leads us to tell people what they want to hear instead of speaking our truth. It's important to stand firm in our beliefs and express disagreements constructively to build true trust. Don't compromise your values to please others. Let your principles guide you, and earn the trust and respect you deserve.

Show Consistency

Building trust requires unwavering consistency. It's a daily commitment, not a one-time gesture. Just as we wouldn't trust a one-star hotel with a fleeting five-star review, our colleagues won't trust us if we're inconsistent. Sustained efforts count. If we want our colleagues to trust us, we need to consistently deliver on our promises and always be truthful. Consistency cultivates trust and influence.

PILLAR 2: LOGIC

To build credibility and trust with our colleagues, it's crucial to consistently demonstrate our expertise, judgment, and reliability. This involves proving our competence through our actions and the information we share and being dependable and valuable contributors to the team.

Herein lies the challenge. Sometimes, our lack of effective communication can erode trust and make our ideas seem less credible. In such instances, it's essential to ground ideas in evidence, speak clearly and concisely, and be truthful about our limitations. Such honesty and humility builds our credibility.

It's common for people to hesitate to advocate for themselves due to a fear of coming across as self-centered, especially for those taught to be humble. We can't just assume that our work will speak for itself. Colleagues can't accurately assess our competence based solely on surface-level observations, so it's imperative that we speak up and demonstrate our expertise to build trust.

The following strategies help you be more credible.

Take Credit for Your Achievements

Own your achievements and abilities without downplaying them. By taking credit for your hard work, you build credibility and trust with colleagues. Accurately represent yourself and confidently acknowledge your success. Taking ownership of your accomplishments is crucial for career advancement, promotions, salary increases, and future opportunities. Additionally, showcase your knowledge and expertise by leading discussions, tackling projects that highlight your strengths, and making impactful contributions during team meetings to build trust in your abilities.

Stay Rigorous in Your Work

To succeed in our careers, we must uphold high standards, deliver quality work, meet deadlines, pay attention to detail, avoid shortcuts, and present well-researched ideas. Consistently delivering our best demonstrates our dedication to excellence and integrity.

Professionalism and respect for our work and colleagues are crucial. Engaging in unprofessional behavior makes us appear lazy and incompetent, undermining our credibility. To earn trust in our capabilities, we must approach our work with diligence, consistently delivering accurate information, tackling problems with a critical mindset, effectively communicating our ideas, and managing our time to meet deadlines with high-quality output.

Be Transparent

Stop hoarding information or keeping secrets at work. It undermines trust. Be transparent, communicate openly, and share regular project updates. Document successes, challenges, key learnings, and collaboration ideas. Share this information at meetings to enhance teamwork.

It's important to always be honest and transparent with your colleagues. Lies, however small, can damage trust and credibility. Leading with transparency can create a culture of openness and support, reducing workplace stress and building stronger, more trusting relationships among team members.

Solicit Feedback

In today's fast-paced workplaces, it's crucial to showcase our unique selling point to stand out; however, trust isn't built by going solo or pretending to know everything. Being a great team player and actively seeking feedback from colleagues is key to earning trust and honing our skills. That's why "feedback" is a recurring theme in this book—it's essential for developing a range of skills.

Asking for help at work makes colleagues feel valued, strengthens connections, and boosts confidence. It's a catalyst for teamwork and enables others to see our strengths. Seeking feedback is helpful in recalibrating objectives, adjusting behavior, and building trust. When receiving feedback, stay open-minded and avoid defensiveness. Embrace constructive criticism, and use it to create an action plan for improvement. This approach fosters honest dialogue and leadership competencies.

Dress the Part

Our perceived credibility and status affect our place in the workplace and society. Studies show that others judge our trustworthiness based on our appearance in less than a second. Dressing well can project confidence and competence, elevating our social status and leaving others with a positive impression of us. Professional attire demonstrates respect for our work and colleagues and reflects our self-respect and values.

Being sloppily dressed or wearing the "wrong" attire can give the impression of laziness, unprofessionalism, and unreliability. This might hinder you from being assigned important work responsibilities. Paying attention to our appearance and attire enhances our credibility and trustworthiness.

PILLAR 3: EMPATHY

It's important to be empathetic in order to build trust. If people perceive us as self-centered and lacking in compassion, they won't trust us. For instance, multitasking on our phones while someone is talking or being unforgiving of others' mistakes can come off as insensitive. It's essential to show empathy toward others' struggles and avoid seeming self-righteous.

Not taking the time to make personal connections at work can make coworkers perceive us as less empathetic. Research from Harvard Business School shows that high achievers often struggle with this, as their drive for productivity can make them impatient with team members who need more time.[23] This is also a challenge for analytical people who become frustrated when others require more time to understand new concepts. However, it's possible to develop deeper empathy and improve relationships with colleagues.

The following strategies help you be more empathetic.

Be Emotionally Aware

To understand others' emotions, we must first understand our own. This is key for building empathy. As we discussed in Chapter 2, we must become aware of our emotions such as sadness, disappointment, and fear to truly grasp what others are feeling. This enables us to support them without judgment because we've experienced similar emotions.

Recognizing and managing our emotions helps us maintain professionalism in our interactions. Unresolved emotions from other issues can lead to erratic behavior toward undeserving colleagues, creating a sense of unease and breaking down trust. Expressing our emotions not only humanizes us but also fosters connections with others, as communicating how we are feeling gives others the opportunity to show us empathy.

Stay Engaged

Are you fully engaged, actively listening, and asking insightful questions when a colleague is explaining something directly to you or during a team meeting? People who lack empathy tend to make everything about themselves, often disengaging or showing disinterest when others are speaking. It becomes difficult for our colleagues to like or trust us when our behavior shows that we think we are more important than everyone else.

To deepen your empathy, actively listen to others. In team meetings, stay fully engaged until each person has shared their thoughts. Minimize distractions and be present, generous, and respectful to build trust.

Show Appreciation for Others

Recognizing and valuing others is fundamental for creating strong relationships. It reflects our character and makes others feel appreciated. Small acts, such as remembering a colleague's birthday or acknowledging their achievements, can have a significant impact, boosting morale and fostering a culture of support in the workplace.

Don't forget to appreciate your colleagues. While you should do this as a matter of course, know that it's also important for your career progression to be seen as a team player. Small actions such as checking in on them, thanking them for their efforts, or offering to grab them a coffee can go a long way in building trust and strengthening professional relationships.

Offer Support

Empathetic individuals have the remarkable ability to support others with innate kindness. By recognizing when a team member is struggling and offering to help, we strengthen our role as valuable team players and build deeper connections with our colleagues. Alleviating workload or offering advice demonstrates empathy and builds trust.

Consistently practicing these small, empathetic gestures cultivates a culture of support and collaboration for all.

When offering support to colleagues, always ask if they need assistance first. Don't impose your help on them. Taking care of yourself is essential, so be cautious of overextending yourself to avoid burnout.

Learn to Forgive

How can we find the courage to forgive when our colleagues or managers unintentionally offend or upset us? Forgiving without empathy is incredibly challenging. Empathy allows us to understand why someone may have betrayed us. It enables us to humanize the person and consider the possibility that their betrayal may have stemmed from their own struggles rather than from malice. Understanding these motivations can lead us to act compassionately and forgive.

Forgiveness requires us to objectively assess how we might have caused any hurt, and consider how we'd like to be treated when we let others down. It's mature, introspective work, but it can repair trust and free us from pain and suffering.

WAYS TO ASSESS YOUR TRUST GAP

To build trust, we need to become more self-aware of how others perceive our trustworthiness. Start by identifying where you may be faltering in the three aspects of trust. Use the following exercises to evaluate your trust gap, and then use the strategies outlined in this chapter to close the gap.

Exercise 1

1. Recall a recent work situation where you felt you weren't trusted as much as you could have been, leading to a missed opportunity, failed deal, promotion oversight, or being undermined by a colleague.
2. Consider the valid reasons your colleague may not have trusted you. Take ownership to determine which aspect of trust faltered. Identify whether you were being authentic, credible, or empathetic and if you mispresented yourself or your story, failed to rigorously vet your idea, or put your own interests first.
3. Repeat the assessment with two or three other incidents. Identify any consistent patterns, and check whether they are affected by stress or other variables.

Exercise 2

Consider asking the colleague involved to share their perspective on what's causing the loss of trust. Their feedback may be hard to hear, but it can help you better understand yourself and find a resolution. If this feels too daunting, stick with the self-assessment exercise.

5

HOW TO SET BOUNDARIES

Our modern workplaces are increasingly becoming a breeding ground for stress and anxiety. The pressure to do more with less, combined with the expectation to be available 24/7 due to technology and remote work, has blurred the lines between work and personal life. This relentless pressure is driving 80 percent of employees to experience stress at work, with 25 percent ranking work as their top source of stress, according to the American Psychiatric Association's (APA) annual mental health poll in 2024.[24] The result? Many of us are teetering on the edge of burnout.

Establishing clear boundaries is crucial for protecting our well-being. Only by defining our limits can we ensure that we prioritize what truly matters and maintain a healthy balance in our lives. The following personal story serves as a cautionary tale, illustrating the repercussions of neglecting to establish clear boundaries and safeguard our physical and mental well-being. The narrative anchors the chapter, offering impactful strategies for setting boundaries while minimizing potential retaliation.

HUMAN SKILLS

It's early 2018, and I'm home alone in downtown Manhattan, working at my kitchen table. The clock on my computer reads 3:35 a.m. The city is unusually quiet and feels eerie, like a ghost town. No wailing police sirens, no screeching garbage trucks, no honking cabs. Nothing. Outside my window, fine snow falls and clings to the barren trees like powdered sugar. I'm fatigued and sleep-deprived. With my husband away traveling, I must have completely lost track of time, buried in my work.

Earlier this month, our team at the United Nations helped to facilitate groundbreaking legislation in Iceland, making it the first country in the world to make equal pay a law. My boss is keen for us to use this momentum to engage more countries to do the same, including here in the US, where unequal pay is still prevalent due to the absence of a federal policy. The pressure is on. We must strike while the iron is still hot, and there aren't enough hours in the day. It's my third night in a row working to finalize the proposal to be presented to policymakers.

My eyes feel heavy with sleep. I get up to fetch a refreshing glass of water from the fridge when suddenly there is banging on my door—*boom, boom ... boom, boom*—a dull, heavy sound like a hammer hitting a concrete wall. I'm not expecting anyone. I freeze in my tracks, and cold, prickly sweat gathers at the nape of my neck. *Boom, boom ... boom, boom;* I hear the sound again. A sharp pain shoots across my chest, creating a heaviness as if an elephant is sitting on it. I know I'm breathing, but it doesn't feel like it. *Stay calm and breathe,* I whisper to myself, drawing in rapid, short breaths, which only makes me lightheaded. I know I must sit down, but I'm paralyzed with fear; I can no longer move my legs.

Boom, boom ... boom, boom—the sound persists, so forceful it causes the windows to rattle. *Boom, boom ... boom, boom.* I shut my eyes and cover my ears, but the sound grows louder. My heart is now pounding a million miles a minute, as adrenaline courses through my veins. *Boom, boom ... boom, boom. Think,* I say to myself, drawing in a sharp breath, trying to still my mind. I remember this sound. I remember this feeling. The pounding isn't coming from my door. It's my heart, telling me that something is terribly wrong. I clench my jaw and brace for the worst.

First, there is a loud bang in my ears. Then, the floor beneath my feet begins to crumble like a sandcastle hit by a tidal wave. My knees buckle, and I land on the ground with a thump. I'm sinking to the bottom of a deep, dark hole. There is no air, no light, and no way out. I try standing but can't move from the ground. The walls of the hole continue to crumble, closing in on me. I feel a burning sensation travel through my body like hot lava; my lungs collapse like a deflated balloon; my head rings with pain. *You're having a heart attack. You're dying,* I think, feeling hot tears sting my eyes.

When I open my eyes, I'm lying on my kitchen floor. Sitting next to me is my friend Vanessa, looking at me with tearful brown eyes. Her curly afro hair, bundled at the top of her head, is wrapped in a floral headscarf, accentuating her long, slender face. She is wearing gray pajamas and thick black socks. I try to think what happened, but my mind is too slow to process.

"There she is. How are you feeling? You had another panic attack, but you're going to be okay." Her words fill in the details of my confused state, as she helps me sit up.

"I'm so glad you called," she continues, holding a glass of cold water to my lips.

I don't remember calling Vanessa. Even though she has a spare key to my apartment, I don't remember hearing her come in at all.

"You okay?" She carefully examines my face with the precision of a surgeon performing a life-saving operation.

I'm still lightheaded but can breathe normally, so I nod, sipping water to soothe my parched throat.

"That's good because we need to have another tough talk, E." She shakes her head. You remember what you promised last time, right?"

she asks intensely.

Vanessa is the kind of friend who nurtures me but also gives me tough love. Still, her question makes me tense, reminding me of an incident I would much rather forget—my very first panic attack, a few years earlier.

It was early 2015, just before the World Economic Forum held yearly in Davos, Switzerland. I was scheduled to participate with the United Nations secretary general and United Nations goodwill ambassador and British actress Emma Watson to launch an initiative for world leaders and Fortune 500 CEOs to champion bold commitments to advance gender equality in their countries and institutions. I had been working nonstop preparing for the event when I suddenly suffered what I thought was a heart attack. Rushed to the emergency room, I had medical tests that revealed I was, in fact, having a panic attack, which had been brought on by increased work stress.

"Listen, something has to give. You just can't keep going like this, E," Vanessa lamented when she saw me upon my release from the hospital. "Your workload is nuts, and you can't care for the world's problems if you don't care for yourself first. You've gotta learn to set healthy work boundaries. Trust me, I know what I'm talking about," she continued, mincing no words.

She was right. As an occupational psychologist for a global energy company in Manhattan, she not only understood the importance of mental health but had suffered her share of work-related health crises, including a miscarriage. But I didn't heed Vanessa's advice nor listen to my doctor's order to reduce stress and prioritize my mental health. Even though I felt physically and emotionally drained the morning following the panic attack, I boarded a plane to the World Economic Forum. *How could I take time off when there is so much work to be done?* I asked myself that morning. How could I cancel such an important engagement? In the face of so many injustices in the world, worrying about my mental health seemed unnecessary, if not self-absorbed. Because of my work on gender equality, I knew that there were millions of women and girls across the world experiencing far more unbearable suffering.

However, as I sit in my apartment on this cold winter morning with Vanessa, I can't help but blame myself. Despite the insistence of my doctor to reduce my work stress, and the numerous pleas from my friends and family to prioritize my own health, I've done no such thing.

"What now?" Vanessa asks as she throws a linen blanket over my shivering body and helps me settle onto the couch.

I have no idea how to respond to her, so I say nothing and avert my eyes to the floor, disappearing into my own small world. I reflect on the significant sacrifices I've made over the decades for my job: my health, marriage, and family. I think about the countless dinners, family vacations, and holidays I have missed in order to attend to a work crisis or last-minute project deadline. I think about the numerous occasions when I have accepted every new assignment from my boss with a smile, when I should have pushed back or asked for additional support. I reflect on the many times I have felt overstretched, burnt out, and unappreciated in my job, yet I failed to communicate my needs or set healthy boundaries. As these memories fill my head, a sense of melancholy envelopes me like a dark cloud.

For most of my professional life, I have held high-level positions and believed that achieving a healthy work-life balance was impossible in the demanding world of work. I thought that as a woman in prominent executive roles, I needed to emulate the stoic demeanor of male leaders. Looking back on my experiences, I realized that I had wrongly believed personal matters had no place in the professional sphere. As a result, I complied and went the extra mile, often tolerating behaviors from superiors and colleagues that exploited my goodwill and trust.

I felt grateful for the opportunity to address global issues with top decision-makers and believed that my personal sacrifices were necessary to make a meaningful impact. As a minority leader, I also carried the weight of representing my community and the responsibility to avoid missteps that could affect other minorities.

After experiencing painful personal losses, I realized the importance of integrating my work and personal life. I found that achieving a balance between the two was crucial for my well-being and professional fulfillment. I began prioritizing myself, setting boundaries, and communicating my needs at work. I discovered that work-life balance is essential for both the well-being of individuals and organizational success, and it has influenced my approach to leadership. I now advocate for a more balanced and sustainable work culture where personal well-being is valued alongside professional achievement.

WHY WE NEED BOUNDARIES

Many of us can relate to the daily personal sacrifices we make, often prioritizing work over other important aspects of our lives. It's a common struggle to find a healthy work-life balance, with most of us so consumed by work that we don't realize the toll it's taking on our well-being until it's too late. This widespread work stress has become a major concern for the World Health Organization, prompting the development of evidence-based guidelines on mental well-being in the workplace.[25]

It's crucial to acknowledge that despite the various pressures we face, we are not machines; we are human beings who need good health and well-being to perform at our best. Setting clear boundaries is essential for our well-being, as continuously pushing ourselves beyond our limits will lead to serious health consequences. Without addressing this, our situation will not improve, and we will end up harming ourselves.

Having clear boundaries empowers us to protect our physical, mental, and emotional well-being, especially in demanding jobs. Boundaries give us a sense of autonomy and enable us to articulate our needs to our colleagues, fostering mutually respectful relationships. This involves outlining what we deem acceptable in terms of behavior and communication expectations and defining parameters for interaction. Since we are all unique, it's crucial to communicate our boundaries openly to create a work environment where everyone feels secure and respected.

This scenario may sound familiar to some of us. Imagine that you've committed to going to the gym after work, but your manager drops an urgent request on your desk right as you're preparing to leave. By the time you're done, it's nearly 7:00 p.m. You're too tired to work out, and you've missed dinner. After a long commute, you have a bland microwave meal and get another urgent email from your manager as you're settling down for bed. If you don't set firm boundaries, this cycle will continue.

In some workplaces, we may face pressure to work long hours and forgo setting boundaries. Reporting this behavior to HR could lead to backlash. While we may not change our colleagues' practices, we can take control by setting our boundaries without causing conflict, starting with examining our own actions.

Be mindful of how your actions can affect boundaries. For example, answering messages after work hours gives the impression you are always available, leading to disappointment when you're not responsive. Also, being the only one to respond to a non-urgent message from your boss in a group chat can create resentment among your colleagues. This might make them feel pressured to prioritize work over personal time in order to match your level of responsiveness.

Equally, sending nonurgent messages to colleagues after work hours is disrespectful and can lead to a lack of mutual respect for boundaries. Messaging your boss after working hours is also inappropriate. Unless absolutely necessary, it invades their personal time and may lead to a loss of respect. If it's nonurgent, get their approval before contacting them.

As a leader, it's important to respect your team's personal time by avoiding after-hours communication and expecting immediate responses. This shows that you value their well-being and work-life balance. Lead by example, and set boundaries for communication.

ESTABLISHING BOUNDARIES

Establishing work boundaries requires more than just defining our limits. We need to effectively assert ourselves to protect our personal time, push back on extra work, and safeguard our well-deserved breaks and vacations. There are three crucial steps to establishing work boundaries:

Step 1: Define Your Priorities

Identify your priorities, and set boundaries accordingly. If family time is important, limit work outside regular hours. Make time for family commitments within your schedule. Setting boundaries safeguards well-being and helps you excel in your career. Say no to new requests until current tasks are complete. Prioritize tasks based on your career goals and key performance indicators (KPIs). Consider investing time in upskilling over taking on more requests from your boss.

Step 2: Communicate Your Boundaries

Once you've set your boundaries, communicate them effectively with your manager and colleagues. Introduce one boundary at a time to avoid overwhelming others. When communicating a boundary, focus on the organizational impact. For example, if your manager assigns too much work, discuss the impact on project timelines and suggest prioritization, instead of complaining about it. Implement boundaries effectively and adjust as necessary. For instance, if you've set a boundary to protect your personal time after work, avoid consistently working late. Maintain a respectful and professional demeanor to convey your message effectively.

Step 3: Enforce Your Boundaries

Remember, when your boundaries are tested or violated, view it as a chance to improve your boundary-setting skills. Stay calm and assertive, restate your boundary, explain the breach, and specify the consequences for future violations. For example: "I can't take work calls after 8:00 p.m. as this time is for my family. If nonurgent calls continue after hours, I may ignore them until the next day." For a more diplomatic approach with your superiors, you can state: "I request to end work calls after 8:00 p.m. to spend quality time with my family during dinner. I will address urgent matters at the end of each workday before leaving the office."

Respect your boundaries, and communicate empathically with your coworkers. If they continue to violate your boundaries, limit your responsiveness and document all violations for formal filing with management or HR. Consider your role and responsibilities when addressing after-hours availability.

Now that we know the significance of boundaries and how to set them, how do we put them into practice? This section identifies common challenging workplace scenarios and provides effective solutions and approaches for overcoming them.

HUMAN SKILLS

WAYS TO CREATE BOUNDARIES AROUND COMMUNICATION

When a boss or coworker contacts us after hours, it's stressful and can make us feel powerless. Seeing their name pop up can trigger anxiety. We all need personal time to relax and recharge for work. Emergencies may arise, but working after hours should be the exception rather than the rule.

Switch Off
Remember to set clear boundaries with work-related communications. Power down your phone, or adjust the focus settings after work. Consider setting up a polite voicemail message for after-hours calls, similar to an out-of-office notification for emails—for instance, "Thank you for calling. You've reached me after hours. Please leave a message, and I will get back to you during the next business day between 9:00 a.m. and 5:00 p.m."

Don't Pick Up
Don't reward your boss or coworker for crossing your boundaries by answering your phone. If it's urgent, they will leave a voicemail. Check it at your convenience, and return the call if needed. If it's not urgent, wait until the next business day to respond.

Reinforce
When criticized for not answering your phone, confidently communicate that you prioritize a healthy work-life balance to excel in both personal and professional spheres. For example, "While I'm fully dedicated to my job, I also strive to maintain 100 percent commitment to my personal life outside of working hours. Therefore, I kindly request that urgent matters be addressed during office hours." Even in a role requiring flexibility, it's essential to establish boundaries. For example, "When I finish work, my focus shifts to my family or personal

obligations. If an urgent situation arises, I will check my phone at 8:00 pm; otherwise, I will address it during business hours the next day."

Key considerations: If you work in a unsupportive environment, a more practical approach is to establish "flexible boundaries" by clearly communicating your availability after work hours. For instance, your message might state: "I will have limited access to communication as I will be traveling over the weekend, but I will respond to urgent messages as soon as possible"; or, "I have an important dinner tonight, so while I won't be available for calls or texts, I will respond to urgent emails after dinner"; or, "I will be attending to an important personal matter on Saturday and will be unavailable." The more specific you are, without compromising your privacy, the more effective your explanation will be.

If your flexible boundaries are being ignored, it's helpful to respond promptly to minimize any anxiety for you and your manager or coworker. For instance, if you receive a message at 10:00 p.m. asking you to contact a coworker for a report, replying with, "I'll reach out to her when I'm in the office and will get back to you before 10:00 a.m." shows your proactive approach and sets a realistic timeframe.

If the work culture won't change, consider finding a new job if possible. We only live once, and our well-being matters more than our job or money.

WAYS TO CREATE BOUNDARIES AROUND MESSAGING

Since we now communicate across an ever-expanding range of channels and platforms, establishing messaging boundaries requires self-awareness and effective prioritization. Avoid feeling pressured to work outside of regular hours, but use your judgment when necessary. If working in a global team, consider different time zones, flexible working hours, and respect for everyone's time off. Create clear prioritization criteria for messages received after hours to simplify decision-making. Consider the following categories:

1. Urgent

These messages require immediate attention, such as inquiries from clients or bosses. Use discretion when labeling messages as urgent. If you regularly receive urgent messages outside of working hours, discuss this with your supervisor to reassess your boundaries.

2. Feedback

These messages may require your input or feedback, possibly from your boss or colleagues seeking your guidance on a project or in making decisions. Address them during work hours. If not responding would stress you out, reply promptly for your well-being. Avoid making immediate feedback a habit. If your workload hampers completion of essential tasks during official hours, discuss with your manager to reprioritize.

3. Acknowledgment

These messages are not urgent and only require an acknowledgment of receipt. They can typically wait until the next business day. This helps convey to your colleagues that nonurgent messages are not answered after hours.

Key considerations: To accommodate different time zones in a global team, consider adding a note in your email signature explaining your flexible work hours. For example, you can mention that you may send emails outside of regular hours but don't expect immediate responses. If you prefer working after hours, schedule your emails to be sent at the start of the next workday, or save them as drafts to send during business hours.

WAYS TO CREATE BOUNDARIES FOR TIME OFF

Our time off should be work-free. It's important for our well-being, but coworkers often disrupt it with work-related messages. To prevent this, we need to communicate clearly before our vacation to set boundaries and promote mutual respect for each other's time off.

Plan Ahead and Delegate

Your vacation is important, but it shouldn't disrupt work. Remember to enter your vacation days into the company's system and get approval from your supervisor. Consider project milestones and events before scheduling your time off, then communicate your holiday schedule to your coworkers in advance. Provide details of your backup coworker, and include this information in your out-of-office messages. Before leaving, complete urgent tasks and prepare a handover document for your backup. Communicate your availability to your boss and coworkers, and let them know you'll respond to urgent matters that can't be handled by your backup within twenty-four hours.

Firmly Address Requests

Despite your careful planning, if your colleagues still contact you during your vacation, assess the urgency of their messages. If it can wait or be handled by your backup, delegate or postpone it. If not, respond assertively, reminding them that you're on vacation: "As you know, I'm currently on vacation and will be back in the office on [date]. Here's the requested information. I'm looking forward to truly disconnecting and recharging during my vacation, so that I can return refreshed and rejuvenated. In the meantime, [name] will be available to assist. Thank you for your understanding."

Have a Postmortem

When you return to the office, it's important to have a postmortem conversation with your coworkers. This is a chance to give them feedback on any work-related challenges that arose during your vacation. If your coworkers respected your time off, express gratitude and commit to doing the same for them. If they didn't, have an open discussion about what went wrong, and take responsibility where needed. Evaluate whether you chose the right backup, provided sufficient handover notes, and completed urgent tasks before leaving. Ask for feedback on how to improve your planning and delegation for future vacations.

WAYS TO CREATE BOUNDARIES WITH WORKLOAD

It's important to assert ourselves and communicate openly with colleagues and superiors, especially regarding managing workload and preventing burnout. Navigating these conversations can be tough, but there are effective strategies for setting and maintaining boundaries without outright refusal.

Realign on Priorities

Discuss your current workload with your boss or coworker before taking on more tasks. Show them your detailed workload plan, including ongoing projects, timelines, and delivery dates. Clearly explain how taking on extra work will affect your current projects. Ask for help to deprioritize or reassign tasks as needed. When taking on a new task, clearly define the scope, timeline, and delivery date. Ensure they are reasonable and won't encroach on your personal time. Set boundaries and make it clear how you want to be treated to avoid others taking advantage of you. Place the responsibility on them to learn how to prioritize effectively and not overload you with tasks.

Don't Complain; Offer Solutions

When your boss gives you too much work because you're the most competent team member, take charge. Instead of carrying the load alone, suggest ways to involve the rest of the team. Brainstorm solutions to share the workload, such as supporting a coworker in leading the project or creating a project team. By presenting solutions, you showcase your leadership and problem-solving skills. When declining additional tasks, emphasize your commitment to delivering quality work, and explain that would be impossible if you're overstretched. Make it clear that you value being on the team and want to continue contributing at your best.

Be Transparent and Proactive

Regularly update your boss on your workload and progress. Communicate specific reasons for feeling overwhelmed, and avoid expressing frustration. This will help your boss consider your workload before assigning new tasks.

WAYS TO REESTABLISH BOUNDARIES AFTER SAYING YES

As humans, we all make mistakes and sometimes find ourselves in situations where we wish we had made a different choice. You may have agreed to lead a new project or accepted an after-work invitation out of fear, politeness, or a mix of anxiety and excitement. Perhaps you felt pressured to say yes, even though you'd rather undergo a root canal than spend time with a certain coworker. You might find it tolerable to interact with them in the office, but the thought of socializing with them fills you with dread. Alternatively, you might have realized that you simply don't have the capacity to take on more work after agreeing to a new project. Now, as you reflect on these decisions, you may feel anxious about the prospect of saying no, fearing that it will damage relationships. Here's how to back out of commitments gracefully.

Know the Cost

Before breaking a commitment, consider potential consequences such as hurting others, damaging your reputation, and missing learning opportunities. Evaluate the pros and cons, and address the underlying reasons for wanting to bail out. Identify whether honoring the commitment will bring substantial gains, and remember that it's acceptable to decline if you feel excessively burdened. Maintain boundaries for self-respect and self-love.

Act Gracefully and Tactfully

While there is no guarantee that your coworker won't be upset if you back out of a commitment, it's crucial to have an honest conversation with them. Handle the dialogue gracefully and tactfully, focusing on what you can confirm. Keep your withdrawal concise and assertive. You might say, "I'm truly sorry. When I confirmed the invitation, I didn't realize the extra hours that I would need to put in to catch up with work," or "Apologies for the cancellation, but I overlooked that I have a personal commitment at the same time." If you genuinely want to make it work later, add, "However, I may be able to find some time to go out in the coming week/month." Only say this if you actually mean it. It's important to avoid giving a litany of excuses in the future if you have no intention of spending time with them, as this will erode trust.

It's okay to be honest if you're uncomfortable socializing with a colleague outside of work. You can say, "I value my professional and personal boundaries, so I usually refrain from socializing with coworkers after hours. However, I'm open to grabbing lunch or coffee during the workday." Remember, building a rapport with your colleagues can greatly benefit your career. Finding opportunities to connect during the workday can still be valuable, and it's important to demonstrate that you're a team player. However, you shouldn't feel obligated to socialize outside of work hours. Your personal time is precious, and it's important to prioritize what matters to you.

When declining a task you've already committed to, it's essential to propose a viable solution to avoid inconveniencing your boss or coworker. You could lead with something such as, "When I initially accepted this assignment, I genuinely believed I could manage the project. However, after reviewing my workload, I've realized it won't be feasible. Nonetheless, I'm committed to facilitating a smooth handover process and will make myself available to participate in the project kickoff meeting." This not only sets your boundary but also demonstrates your dedication to ensuring the project's success.

No matter the circumstances, it's crucial to assert yourself and refuse to be pressured into agreeing to something that could harm your well-being or mental health simply because you previously said yes. While saying no may initially feel uncomfortable, it's far worse to take on something halfheartedly, as your lack of enthusiasm or availability will inevitably become apparent and could lead to a negative outcome. Stand up for yourself, and prioritize your own welfare.

Learn from Your Experience

Setbacks offer valuable lessons. Stepping back from a commitment can provide insight for evaluating future opportunities, prioritizing mental and emotional well-being, and developing leadership qualities such as transparency, time management, and handling challenging conversations. While saying no is sometimes necessary, it's important not to make it a habit to avoid eroding trust. Manage your workload and keep your schedule up to date to prevent overcommitting.

WAYS TO CREATE BOUNDARIES FOR PERSONAL LIFE

Your personal life is off-limits to your coworkers. You have every right to keep it that way. It's in your best interest to do so, as oversharing personal information can jeopardize your credibility and make you vulnerable to judgment, gossip, and biased evaluations. While it's important to be authentic and open with coworkers, it's equally important to preserve your privacy and set clear boundaries.

Be Polite but Direct

Remember, it's okay to be private without being rude. It's important to be professional and respectful when others try to pry into your personal life. Set boundaries and maintain positive relationships with your colleagues. You don't have to share anything that makes you uncomfortable. You can kindly say, "I prefer to keep my personal life separate from work. I hope you can understand and respect that. If you have some time, I would love to get your input on one of the projects I'm working on." Being open about your discomfort is more likely to foster understanding and empathy. This is more effective than just saying, "I don't want to talk about my private life," which might come off as abrupt. Shifting the conversation to work-related topics shows your considerate nature and helps others feel valued. This approach not only keeps personal matters at bay but also avoids potential awkwardness.

If direct communication makes you uncomfortable, a simple response such as, "My personal life is pretty average and not very interesting," may be enough. If someone persists in wanting to know more about you, share unimportant details such as a hobby or upcoming weekend plans, and then steer the conversation back to the other person. People enjoy talking about themselves, so ask them plenty of questions. By actively listening, you can engage in meaningful conversations while safeguarding your personal details.

Avoid Gossiping

Avoiding office gossip can help to protect your privacy and professional reputation. Stick to professional interactions, and set boundaries with gossiping colleagues. For instance, if a colleague remarks, "Did you hear that Jeff is behind on his deliverables again? He really needs to be reprimanded this time," you could respond, "Seems like we're all swamped with work lately. Speaking of which, I've got to dive into it," with a smile before walking away. If they ask, "What do you think about Amy's behavior at the pub last night? She should be ashamed!" you could reply, "Last night was quite a wild ride for everyone. I think we all might have taken it a bit too far."

Another effective diplomatic approach is to focus on the positive traits of your colleagues, such as Jeff's ability to complete projects with limited resources and Amy's ability to bring joy to the team. Refrain from engaging in gossip to discourage others from doing so.

Considerations for social media: Remember that what we share online can affect our professional lives. Colleagues and managers often check our online presence, so if your social media accounts are not private, avoid sharing personal information you wouldn't want them to see. Even small errors in your posts can reflect poorly on your abilities. Keep your social accounts private, or consider having a separate public professional profile to protect your privacy.

6

HOW TO SPEAK UP

Team meetings present a critical opportunity to actively engage, collaborate, and build strong connections with colleagues by speaking up. Demonstrating assertiveness and voicing our thoughts establishes our professional credibility. We can inspire and influence others, advocate for our ideas, and thrive as leaders. Moreover, it's a chance to hone our negotiation skills, ensure all viewpoints are considered, and drive positive change within our workplaces.

With a captive audience, team meetings also serve as a platform to refine our public speaking skills and become exceptional communicators. Unfortunately, many individuals fail to realize the importance of this, ultimately to their own detriment, as we will delve into later in this chapter. Not speaking up perpetuates a culture of silence within your workplace, a reality vividly illustrated by my experience with a group of high-level executives at a Fortune 500 company in London.

The story is followed by valuable strategies for confidently speaking up and effectively expressing your ideas and opinions.

HUMAN SKILLS

In a crowded airport lounge at New York's JFK airport, I hunch over my laptop, researching the names of the people I'm about to meet in London. I scour the internet scrolling through anything I can find: their LinkedIn profiles, social media channels, and wiki pages.

It's remarkable how much information you can glean about a person from their social media. There's Mark, the private type, who only ever shares newspaper articles with minimal personal commentary; Kelly, the self-proclaimed feminist (according to her social bio), who is hyperactive on all things gender equality; and Michael, the corporate guy and dog lover who predominately reshares from the corporate accounts, interspacing the posts with images of his dog Bruno, a black and brown German Shepherd.

After a smooth hop over the Atlantic Ocean, I take a cab to Victoria Embarkment and then a glass elevator to the eleventh floor, glancing out at the Thames River slithering like a shiny snake dividing the city of London. At the end of a long white corridor, I find the small room: bleak and unremarkable, with pasty walls and a tiny closed window looking out to a concrete-grey sky. Two columns of row seating split the room into two; six women occupy the right side, and roughly seventeen men cram on the left. *That's no good,* I think, and put on my game face.

With more than two decades of experience motivating people to adopt positive behavior, I know that a room's layout can impact a group's dynamic. Divided seating, especially when people organize themselves into group of similar types, creates a binary dynamic that can polarize the conversation. Together with the executives, we rearrange the chairs in a circle, and I ask the genders to mix.

The global consumer company has been trying to increase the number of women in its senior leadership for years. Progress has been slow, and the CEO wants me to discuss challenges and identify solutions with his leadership team. There's tension in the air. If resistance was flammable, starting a fire would only take the smallest spark.

According to behavioral psychologist Dr. Albert Mehrabian, 93 percent of human interactions are nonverbal.[26] I search for nonverbal cues to understand the group's emotions and dynamics. I observe a few closed postures, crossed arms indicating defensiveness or self-protection, eyes cast downward to avoid contact, and foot tapping from several men denoting annoyance or impatience, maybe both. I get on with it.

I know that I need to earn the men's trust quickly. In a warm tone, I establish that I'm not here to lecture or judge but rather to learn. Using ego as a motivator, I praise all of the executives for what the company has already achieved.

"You could be a great role model for the industry," I enthusiastically state.

The tactic works, inciting open gestures. A few shoulders drop, several smiles stud the room, and others lean in.

Tom, one of the executives, is a proud father who constantly posts images of his three-year-old daughter on social media. A 2016 Australian study found that male chief executives with daughters are more likely to champion gender diversity.[27] I ask Tom to help me facilitate the conversation and immediately get a cold stare from one of the female executives which says, *Why would you pick a man over a woman?*

My move, however, is intentional. When only women lead the gender conversation in a male-dominated setting, most men disengage, viewing it as a women's issue with nothing or little to do with them.

For the next two hours, Tom and I encourage equal participation to drive ownership. Research on human behavior, including from Harvard Business Review, suggests that people don't respond positively to top-down communication.[28] Thus, we ensure that executives of all genders participate in discussions on each hot-button topic: pipeline development, the hiring process, promotion, and talent retention. The conversation is lively and dynamic.

When leaders participate in problem-solving, they begin to view themselves as diversity champions. So, I probe deeper on identified challenges: why it has been taking so long to increase female representation, why the company has a high attrition rate for female employees compared to men, and why there isn't a clearly defined professional development plan.

Two female executives vocalize their concern about gender biases in the workplace. A few male executives immediately adopt closed postures; their arms fold, and they lean back in their chairs. *They feel attacked.* James, one of the male executives, is a huge Manchester United fan. *He likes team sports; he might value teamwork.* I follow my hunch and ask for his input. He plays ball.

"The challenge is that we are dealing with too many competing priorities," James states. "We have gender issues, then LGBTQI, then minorities—while also being expected to deliver on operations and make money for the company."

His input, though insightful, fails to acknowledge the concerns of the two female executives, one of whom shakes her head and lowers her gaze. The room falls silent.

The next morning, I meet with the CEO. The team wasn't forthcoming with answers, I inform him. "We need a different tactic," I suggest, then ask to hold one-to-one meetings with some executives and general staff. How a company treats its staff is usually a good indicator of its culture.

In private bilateral meetings, the floodgates are pushed wide open, and everyone speaks up. Female executives and staff reveal that the exodus of female employees is due to a "toxic culture that is discriminatory against women." They express frustration over being consistently passed over for promotions and cite the lack of work-life balance, which has led to burnout and anxiety. Meanwhile, male executives and staff also share their concerns, expressing unease about being expected to execute mandates without room for discussion. They question the effectiveness of current inclusion efforts and express the need for open dialogue on how these initiatives will benefit the business.

I absorb it all with a heavy heart, as if the somber London sky has swallowed me whole. When I present my discoveries to the executive team, I pinpoint their biggest obstacle: the reluctance to address crucial issues openly in a group setting. These daunting challenges will only fester and worsen if ignored, yet without open discussion, progress remains at a standstill. This begs the question—*how can we hope for change if we lack the bravery to speak up?*

In a culture clouded by fear and silence, finding the courage to speak up can be daunting. Nevertheless, it's essential to recognize that your voice is your most powerful tool for championing your needs. Failing to speak up can result in a toxic environment, much like the teams I witnessed in London, where suppressed voices led to escalating discontent and a lack of open communication in the workplace.

WHY WE MUST SPEAK UP

It's important to speak up in group settings and team meetings, as remaining silent can have a significant impact on your personal and professional life. Here are four reasons why speaking up is essential.

1. To Advance Our Career

Your silence during team meetings can hinder your career. Managers notice those who actively participate and engage. Your silence may make you less visible, leading to doubts about your competence and commitment. This could limit your career advancement and growth opportunities.

2. To Avoid Being Misunderstood

Silence can carry various meanings. For instance, if you disagree with a proposal during a team meeting, staying silent may not effectively convey your disapproval. It's important to recognize that staying silent might not effectively communicate the message you intend and could potentially result in misunderstandings or disagreements.

Consider this: when your spouse unintentionally hurts your feelings and you give them the silent treatment instead of expressing your emotions, they might not understand what they did wrong. Even those closest to you can struggle to understand your silence, so how can you expect your colleagues to do any better?

3. To Avoid Being Manipulated

Silence isn't universally understood. Your silence may be interpreted in various ways by colleagues, allowing unfair behavior to continue unchallenged. Use your voice to express your thoughts and take control of the narrative, rather than relying on chance. Your boss and colleagues may not always have your best interests at heart and can exploit your silence for their benefit.

I once worked for a company with a great culture until a new project lead was brought in on a one-year contract. Despite his skills, he created a toxic work environment by making drastic changes without consulting us and fostering competition among the team. We were all miserable but took solace in knowing he would be gone within a year.

I was shocked when the director announced that the consultant had been offered a longer-term contract due to outstanding achievements. The consultant had sanctioned three new projects and secured two external partnership agreements in the past twelve months; however, our team had not yet approved any of these achievements, even though the consultant had presented them to us and sought our input during team meetings.

His assumption that our silence meant agreement helped him move forward with his plans unchallenged. We thought we were hurting him, but, in reality, we were only hurting ourselves. This made me realize that silence can be just as impactful as speaking and can easily be manipulated.

4. To Stop Monoculture

Speaking up at work prevents the development of a uniform group of "yes" people, ensures that workplace policies are influenced by a variety of perspectives, and is crucial for the effectiveness of those policies for a diverse workforce. Not speaking up can hinder your success and give away your influence.

WAYS TO SPEAK UP

How can we effectively use our voices within groups? Whether you struggle with difficult topics, feel drowned out in larger meetings, are anxious about speaking in public, or feel hesitant due to your junior position, remember that your perspective is valuable, and your voice deserves to be heard.

When invited to collaborate or attend a team meeting, contribute and make your presence count. Others would benefit from being in your seat, so showcase your expertise and pull your weight.

Develop your voice, choose the right words, master effective delivery, and time your contributions with the following tailored strategies to overcome common challenges in team meetings.

Be Assertive

You may have brilliant ideas and be the sharpest in the room, but if you avoid public speaking, your work may not get the recognition it deserves.

A while ago, my friend Lucy, who is an introvert working at a prestigious law firm in London, faced a tough situation. She teamed up with her outgoing male colleague, Henry, for a high-profile case. They worked well together, with Lucy handling research and preparation while Henry took the lead in presenting their project in team meetings. When it came time for promotions, Henry got all the credit for their successful project. When Lucy confronted her boss about it, he dismissed her claims, stating that she hadn't shown leadership on the project. He had never seen Lucy present the case and thought she was being a sore loser.

Don't let anyone steal the spotlight for your hard work. If presenting solo makes you anxious, invite a colleague to co-present with you, but make it clear that you're the leader. Thorough preparation is key. Arm yourself with information, stay focused, and consider calming techniques such as drinking water, breathing exercises, or sitting in a strategic spot.

Speak at Least Once

In group settings and meetings, it's important to speak at least once. You don't need a groundbreaking idea, but asking a thoughtful question or supporting a colleague can make a difference. Remember the power of body language—sit up straight, maintain eye contact, and exude confidence. Observe assertive colleagues to learn from their communication style. Seek their advice outside the meeting room to improve your communication skills.

If interrupted, assertively say: "Let me finish my point before we discuss yours," or, "I would like to complete what I was saying before we move on to your thoughts."

If you're new to the company, clarify your role and expectations before the meeting. Embrace your fresh perspective, and use it to make innovative contributions and bring new ideas to the table.

If you're in a junior position, you can still make a significant impact. If a conversation is beyond your expertise, use it as a chance to expand your knowledge. Contribute by offering to take meeting notes, which showcases your proactive approach. As the notetaker, you can politely seek validation from senior leaders, showing your commitment to understanding their input. Summarize the agreed outcomes at the meeting's conclusion to leave a lasting impression. If you're not needed as a notetaker, stay engaged through nonverbal cues such as active notetaking, nodding affirmatively, and offering reassuring smiles. Your active involvement will make a meaningful impact.

Speak Up Early

Are you a great listener and team player, but struggle to share your own ideas? Or are you frustrated by inconsiderate colleagues and choose to speak less as a result?

To ensure your ideas are heard and to encourage active engagement, commit to speaking up early in the meeting, ideally within the first five to ten minutes. Most people hesitate to go first, so taking the lead increases your chances of success in getting your ideas across. Speaking early not only ensures that your valuable insights are heard but also relieves the pressure of waiting for your turn. Your early contribution may also inspire others to speak up and contribute, enriching the overall conversation and potentially influencing its direction for the benefit of your project.

Don't worry if someone else speaks first or if the meeting is moving quickly. You can still make a strong impact by contributing at the end. Summarize the meeting's outcome, ask for next steps, or follow up with a colleague who made a relevant point. These actions will help you stand out and show your active engagement.

Add Something Insightful

Feeling hesitant to share your ideas at work? Worried about how others perceive you? Don't let these concerns hold you back. Your ideas matter, and it's important to speak up.

To deliver impactful insights in team meetings, immerse yourself in the topic at hand with thorough research, clarify expectations, plan your active participation, seek input from colleagues, and prepare a compelling presentation if needed. Being well informed makes your input more persuasive and confident.

If you didn't have time to prepare for the meeting, don't worry. Pay attention, take notes, and formulate responses to questions in your head. You don't always have to bring new ideas to the table; supporting your colleagues is equally valuable. Show your interest by acknowledging their contributions: "That's so insightful, Ben; I would love to know more," or, "Mela, how did you work that out? I'm curious about your perspective." This will help you come across as engaged and active even if you're not contributing new ideas.

Fight Imposter Syndrome

Feeling like you don't fit into the culture or that your colleagues don't appreciate you? It might seem like they overlook your contributions and leave you feeling insecure. Maybe you're questioning your place and wondering if it's worth sharing your thoughts and ideas. Feeling unsupported at work can lead to self-doubt and imposter syndrome. A study by KPMG found that 75 percent of senior female executives have experienced imposter syndrome.[29] Remember that you belong in that room and have rightfully earned your place at the table. Your contributions are valued, so own it.

To combat imposter syndrome, connect with colleagues and managers outside of formal meetings. Understand their backgrounds and experiences to discover shared interests and common ground. This humanizes your colleagues, making it easier to see them as equals. Remember, you were hired for a reason; you have just as much to offer as anyone else on the team.

Thus, remember to assert yourself in meetings by confidently joining the conversation when a colleague finishes speaking. Start with, "I really like that idea, and it's sparked another point I'd like to add …" This will help you appear more competent and confident.

If you're struggling to find your voice, try enrolling in public speaking courses or joining a Toastmasters club. You can also watch TED Talks to learn communication and storytelling techniques. Consider starting a speaking group with peers to improve your presentation skills.

PART III

HUMAN SKILLS FOR MASTERING WORKPLACE DIFFERENCES

7

HOW TO TALK ABOUT RACE

Race is an extremely sensitive yet important topic in the workplace. It often leads to uncomfortable silences and avoidance. Many of us are hesitant to broach this topic, fearing pushback and conflict. The very idea of bringing it up can cause overwhelming anxiety and stress. This is compounded by cultural tensions, making discussions feel "charged" and leaving little room for nuanced dialogue. If we are a person of color, we may feel exhausted from constantly having to educate others about race and explain why hurtful behavior deeply affects us. We might even shy away from expressing our discomfort and internalize the pain just to avoid being labeled as "difficult." If we are White, we may be afraid of saying the wrong thing, being misunderstood, or being perceived as ignorant or even racist. We might be anxious that one careless word could harm our reputation or even jeopardize our job. As a result, we may feel the need to limit interactions with colleagues of color in order to avoid causing potential harm or conflict.

It's important to recognize that discussions about race with our colleagues are bound to occur and cannot be avoided. Given that most of us lack the skills to engage in these discussions, it's even more likely that we'll find ourselves in situations where we have to address this topic. All too often, a seemingly harmless chat can veer into sensitive territory, unintentionally causing offense and leaving us wishing we had the tools to navigate these conversations effectively. The following intense discussion between two colleagues I met in Paris as part of my inclusion work, perfectly illustrates this point. This chapter provides the dos and don'ts on how to speak about race for both people of color and White colleagues.

I'm in Paris for a speaking engagement at an inclusion seminar organized by a French insurance company. The event is being held on a river cruise ship sailing along the Seine River. As our boat gracefully sails along the shimmering water, we are treated to breathtaking views of the city's most iconic landmarks: the Eiffel Tower, the Louvre, the Musée d'Orsay, and Notre-Dame. After my speech, I join two colleagues positioned at the far end of the deck: Sandrine, a striking Senegalese woman with intricately braided hair that elegantly accentuates her sculpted cheekbones, and Celine, a petite French woman with a chic brunette pixie cut and a graceful oval-shaped face.

"Thanks for addressing race in your remarks," Sandrine says, making room for me around a tall bistro table.

I rest my sparkling water next to their champagne flutes, which are bubbling with pink fizz.

"It's so sad," Celine chimes in. "All those race issues in America. We are so fortunate here in France. It's definitely not an issue in our company."

"Race is absolutely an issue in our company," Sandrine immediately rebuts.

"No, Sandrine, *ce n'est pas vrai*—that's not true. Sexism, *oui*—yes, but not racism."

"*Oui*, Celine," Sandrine insists, "There is racism in our company, believe me."

I know exactly what I have walked into, so I listen intently.

Celine shrugs, casually sips her cocktail, and says, "*Mais non—* but no, you are just wrong about that.*"

"My God, you are so unaware of your privilege," Sandrine pushes back. "Do you know how hard it is for Black people to get promoted? How—"

"Actually, it's not that difficult," Celine responds bluntly. "Look at you and me; we are on the same level." She scans Sandrine up and down as if qualifying her. "All this diversity talk is now about prioritizing Black people. In fact, I would say that nowadays, it is harder for White women like me to get promoted."

"You have to be kidding me, Celine. How many Black women are in leadership roles, compared to White women … how many—"

"But Sandrine, not everything is about race. There are other reasons why people don't get promoted, and it's not helpful when you people make everything about race."

"You people?!"

"Yes, you Black people!"

Just like that, I'm in the middle of a racial storm.

Fury clouds Sandrine's face. "Oh, us Black people. Do you know how *othering* your words are to me?"

"What's wrong with calling you *Black people*? Black people call us *White people* all the time, and we don't complain." Celine throws her arms in the air. "Okay, what exactly are we supposed to call you then?"

Sandrine gasps. She says nothing and stares into the void. Her silence is excruciating. When she finally speaks, her words are measured and firm. "Listen, Celine; it's not my job to teach you about race. If you really care, put in some effort and do your homework; read a book or watch a show. Us Black people, as you just called us, do everything to learn about your culture just to fit in, just to get by in life. We do our work, and it would be much appreciated if you did yours."

"Please don't be so angry and aggressive," Celine pleads, her voice meek and fragile, "please—"

"Oh, so now I am *aggressive*! What other stereotypes besides being an *angry Black woman* do you want to throw my way, huh?"

"Why are you attacking me?" Celine's lip quivers. "You don't understand, Sandrine, how exhausting it is to tiptoe around Black people, constantly afraid of saying the wrong thing. Afraid of upsetting you, when we're just trying to support you. Why do you make it so difficult?"

Another gasp from Sandrine. This time she turns her eyes toward the sky as if pleading with God for an answer that might get through to Celine. "Okay, so you are exhausted?" she says. "Let me try to explain this to you in the gentlest way possible." She glares at Celine. "You have been working on racial equality for about, what, two seconds, and now you're exhausted? Guess how long I have been dealing with racial injustice? Forty-two years ... every single day of my life. When I wake up each day, do you think I have the privilege of saying, 'You know what? I think I'm just too exhausted to deal with race issues today.'" Sandrine mimics Celine's posh accent as she says this. "No, I don't, and this conversation right here is a reminder that I will never be able to just live without having to deal with racism, especially when racist stuff like this keeps happening."

"Are you saying I'm being racist? I am NOT a racist!" Celine's words are understandably defensive.

In her book *White Fragility*, Dr. Robin DiAngelo, a White author, shares her own experience with racism, stating:

> *I would respond with outrage to any suggestions that I was involved in racism. Of course, the belief would make me feel*

falsely accused of something terrible, and of course, I would want to defend my character ... I came to see that the way we are taught to define racism makes it virtually impossible for White people to understand it. Given our racial insulation, coupled with misinformation, any suggestion that we are complicit in racism is a kind of an unwelcome and insulting shock to the system.[30]

"In fact, I don't see any difference between you and me; I ..." Celine tries to explain, but Sandrine abruptly cuts her off.

"Bravo, Celine, bravo," she jeers, "that's precisely what racists say, 'Oh, I don't see any difference. Oh, I don't see color.' Do you know why they say that? It's because they aren't prepared to put in the work."

On the verge of tears, Sandrine looks up again. She swallows hard to stop them from tumbling down her cheeks. Society's stereotype of the "strong Black woman" means that women of color can't show fragility; instead, they are expected to be strong and self-sacrificing, but they are also cautioned not to get too angry or too forceful—something I know too well.

When Sandrine speaks again, her words land like a plea to the rest of the world. She looks away, shielding her pain from Celine and me. "You don't know how dehumanizing your words are," she says. "I want you to see my color, because it is quintessential to who I am. It's what makes me *me*. I want you to see my humanity and acknowledge my presence."

"You know that's not what I meant," Celine's voice quivers. Then, without realizing it, she does the one thing that most Black women are terrified of; after drawing in a sharp breath, she breaks into tears.

In her seminars on cross-racial interactions, DiAngelo tells fellow White participants to remove themselves from the room should they feel moved to tears, stating that *White tears* "have a powerful impact in this setting, effectively reinscribing rather than ameliorating racism."[31] In other words, when a White woman cries, everything suddenly becomes about her, with everyone rushing to her side to console her.

As expected, the arrival of Celine's tears signals to Sandrine that the argument is over. She places her hand on Celine's shoulder and, with a wounded tone as she fights back her own tears, says, "I am sorry; I didn't mean to upset you."

And just like that, a glamorous evening—a sunset in Paris with chilled bubbly champagne on a fancy cruise—has ended in tears. A perfect evening—nothing short of a scene from a romantic movie—has suddenly becomes a dramatic tragedy.

The irony isn't lost on me.

If you have ever been in Sandrine's position, you understand the profound impact of being singled out based on your race and having your very existence dehumanized. For Celine, the scenario is deeply distressing and inconceivable—a harmless exchange with a coworker turns into an accusation of racism. Regardless of your perspective, it's natural to take these situations personally. Our values and identity are central to who we are as human beings, and any attack on them triggers intense emotions that can quickly escalate.

As daunting as it may seem, it's important to recognize that racial diversity is a vital part of the modern workplace, and many of us may find it challenging to navigate this issue. To create inclusive workplaces where everyone feels valued and respected, we need to equip ourselves with the knowledge and skills to have open and constructive conversations about race. The strategies below help you facilitate these conversations with your colleagues.

WAYS TO TALK ABOUT RACE AS A WHITE PERSON

When discussing race, it's easy to stumble into common pitfalls that only exacerbate the situation. By avoiding the following missteps, you can contribute to a more positive and productive dialogue.

Don't Be Dismissive

When a colleague who is a person of color tells you that something you said or did is racially offensive or that they're experiencing racism, it's crucial to take them seriously. Dismissing their concerns with statements like, "Oh, that's not true," or, "I think you are imagining it," isn't only unhelpful, but it also invalidates their feelings, making the situation worse. It's important to recognize that most people of color have more important issues to deal with than making up experiences of being *othered*. They would rather avoid this difficult conversation if they could. Therefore, acknowledge their perspective and show empathy. Instead of being dismissive, ask clarifying questions such as: "I didn't realize, please tell me more," "Thanks for sharing; how has that impacted you?" or, "I wasn't aware; please help me understand." It's essential to create a safe and open space for honest conversations about race and to actively listen to and learn from others' experiences.

Don't pretend to be agreeable just to avoid the conversation while secretly feeling resentful. Talking about race requires courage, honesty, and humility. It's okay to disagree as long as it is done compassionately. For example, you could say, "I don't personally see things that way; can you share an example of what you mean?" This signals your willingness to learn and engage in a respectful debate.

Don't Be Defensive

If your colleague calls you out for using racially-charged language, it's important not to immediately get defensive and remember that this "race thing" is just as difficult for them as it is for you. Nobody enjoys constantly defending their identity, especially in an environment where they may feel unsupported. Instead of feeling defensive, recognize that even with the best intentions, our words can inadvertently cause harm to others, especially if we are not familiar with their background, culture, or experiences. When that happens, apologize and try to understand why your words had a negative impact. Approach the conversation with honesty and humility. Showing your colleagues that you don't have all the answers creates a space for learning from each other.

Don't Deflect

Remember that saying things like, "It's not about race," can feel disempowering and cause a lot of shame. Most people of color also don't want it to be about race, but unfortunately, sometimes it is. No one likes feeling like a victim or being made to feel like an outsider.

Similarly, avoid saying, "I'm tired of talking about race." Yes, we're all tired of it, but racism keeps happening, and not everyone has the luxury of giving up. Such remarks can be diminishing and hurtful. Instead, seek to understand and offer support: "It doesn't seem like what I'm doing is helping; in what other ways can I be a better ally?"

It's crucial to remember that saying, "I don't see color," or, "I'm colorblind," in an attempt to appear less racist can actually have the opposite effect. Your colleague sees your color, and they know that you see theirs; pretending otherwise does not fool anyone. It's important to acknowledge that we all naturally notice race and physical attributes, and denying this comes across as disingenuous and can be hurtful. Rather than signaling the absence of racial prejudices, these statements are actually diminishing to others. They fail to acknowledge the lived experiences of people of color and the continued existence of racial bias and injustice. By recognizing that the world is still unequal and truly understanding the struggle for racial equality, we can strive to be more empathetic and supportive.

Don't Compare

Don't compare your struggles to those of your colleagues. Don't say, "I know exactly how you feel." While it's true that everyone has endured pain and suffering in different ways, each person's experiences are unique. Your struggles aren't precisely the same as your colleagues, and vice versa. Making such comparisons is not only insensitive but also diminishes the significance of their experiences. Remember, it's not always about you.

Avoid using othering language such as "you people," "your kind," or "those people," as it can be seen as divisive and disrespectful. Referring to a group in this way creates an us-versus-them dynamic that hinders open communication. Furthermore, refrain from making it personal by labeling others as "overly sensitive" or "aggressive." Such words can come across as a personal attack and may cause your colleague to shut down. It's crucial to maintain a constructive dialogue by respecting the validity of your colleague's feelings and focusing on the issue at hand, not on their identity or emotions. Try to put yourself in your colleague's shoes, and consider that their perspective might be valid, rather than dismissing their emotions simply because they differ from your own.

WAYS TO TALK ABOUT RACE AS A PERSON OF COLOR

If your colleague makes a racial blunder, it's important to approach the situation thoughtfully. By avoiding the following, you can create a more positive and productive dialogue.

Don't Be Quick to Judge

While words can be hurtful, it's crucial to recognize that discussions about race can be complex and nuanced. Instead of reacting impulsively, consider the intention behind the words. Rather than jumping to conclusions, strive to understand if the mistake was made with genuine ignorance or malice. We all have our blind spots, and it's essential to give others the benefit of the doubt while holding them accountable for their actions.

Don't be quick to judge, but instead ask clarifying questions such as, "Could you help me understand what you mean by that? I might have misunderstood," or, "It sounds like you're trying to communicate something important; could you please clarify?" If someone's words have affected you, be open and honest by initiating a dialogue: "I'm sure you didn't intend to hurt me, but I feel upset by what you said," or, "If you'll allow me, I'd like to explain why that hurt me."

Don't Be Dismissive of Support

If your White colleague wants to offer support or speak out against racial injustice in the workplace, don't assume they have a hidden agenda. Don't accuse them of being a "White savior" or hijacking the race agenda. Perhaps they've simply become more aware of these injustices and genuinely want to help. There are thoughtful and well-intentioned people who want to be allies, and their support is vital. Ending inequality requires solidarity and allyship. It's not solely the responsibility of minorities and marginalized individuals to overcome these barriers, especially when those with more privilege and power can play a crucial role in dismantling them.

When discussing race with your White colleagues, don't immediately label their emotions as "White fragility." If they become emotional during the conversation and "make it all about them," consider challenging your assumptions and giving them the benefit of the doubt. It's entirely possible that their tears stem from genuine remorse for unintentionally causing pain or from a place of deep shame for their actions. People cry for numerous reasons, and it's not fair to jump to conclusions. Certain situations can provoke strong emotions, regardless of our intentions. That doesn't make us racist, or manipulative, or victim-seeking; it just makes us human.

If they ask you to explain something they don't understand, acknowledge their efforts. Don't say, "I can't keep explaining these things to you." Instead, show patience and understanding. Remember, it takes months, if not years, to be fluent in a new language, and the topic of race has its own complex vocabulary. You've likely been discussing race and racism much longer than your colleague, if not your entire life. Recognize their good intentions and willingness to learn. If possible, use encouraging statements such as: "I know this isn't easy, so I appreciate your willingness to know more; I hope I can equally be brave in discussing issues that impact you." Or, "I appreciate you for not shutting down and allowing me to share my perspective. I hope it provides a better understanding."

Don't Jump to Conclusions

Workplace conflicts and personality clashes can have various roots beyond race. Thus, don't assume that every statement is "racially charged" or every criticism is rooted in racism. We all make mistakes, and it's natural for our colleagues to notice and point them out. Sometimes, a colleague might simply not like you, and that's okay. It's a fact of life. I'm sure you don't like everyone you meet.

Don't minimize your colleague's struggles by making everything about "White privilege." While it's true that they may benefit from certain privileges, it's essential to recognize that life presents challenges to everyone. Their hardships are real, regardless of how trivial they may appear to you. Moreover, privilege is not always readily apparent to those who possess it, and it might not fully encompass their individual experiences. Bringing up privilege during a tense conversation will only escalate the conflict and discredit their hard work and achievements, which is unjust.

Don't blame your White colleagues for the actions of their ancestors. After all, none of us can change the past, but we can work together to shape a better future.

WAYS TO INCREASE RACIAL AWARENESS

We all have a race, and that includes White people. Avoiding conversations about race only perpetuates a culture of silence. While these discussions can be uncomfortable, they are essential for navigating our diverse workplaces. Embracing open dialogue not only strengthens relationships with colleagues but also has the potential to drive real change and transform team culture.

In order to truly embrace discussions about race, we must make the effort to educate ourselves. There will undoubtedly be occasions when we have to tackle this topic, so it's crucial to expand our vocabulary. One impactful way to achieve this is by establishing connections with colleagues from diverse racial, cultural, and ethnic backgrounds. If you don't live in a diverse neighborhood, actively seek opportunities to engage with people from different backgrounds at their community and religious events. Moreover, learn about race issues by exploring content created by individuals of color, whether books, podcasts, or other entertainment. By being exposed to diverse voices, you can expand your perspective. Keep in mind, this is a journey. You won't resolve all your uncertainties about race in one conversation. Addressing race-related issues requires ongoing curiosity and dialogue. The more openly you discuss race with your colleagues, the more trust you'll build. The more effort you put in, the easier it will become. As you learn, you'll also grow.

8

HOW TO BRIDGE THE GENERATION GAP

In today's workplaces, age diversity is the new norm, with members from four to five different generations—Gen Z, younger Millennials, older Millennials, Gen X, and younger Baby Boomers. Despite the opportunity for skill exchange and varied perspectives, in a study by the Society of Human Resource Management, 60 percent of workers report experiencing generational conflict at work.[32] These conflicts typically arise from clashes over values, work styles, expectations, and communication. To address these challenges, it's crucial to have the human skills to navigate our differences with patience and understanding, even in the most difficult situations. I'll share a story of a tense conversation I had with a young activist during a high-level event in Egypt, to illustrate this point, followed by effective strategies for bridging the multigenerational gap in the workplace.

―――

I weave through hordes of people in the Egyptian desert, my feet kicking up puffs of dust, my shoulders slicing through the crowds like a hot knife through butter. The month is November, 2022. The location, Sharm El-Sheikh. The temperature, a sweltering 144 degrees Fahrenheit—hot enough to fry an egg and wilt my long white dress, which snakes, limp with sweat, around my ankles.

I hurriedly negotiate the narrow pathways, dodging between massive, corrugated steel structures and chanting youth protestors, past a food courtyard where sweaty vendors sell soggy sandwiches, and around a group of impeccably dressed African men—until I reach a white canopy tucked behind the buildings, which serves as a retreat away from the crowds. Suddenly, I notice her—the petite girl, roughly in her early twenties, with bright-pink pixie hair, following me. I instantly recognize her, and dread fills me.

"What are you doing here?" she asserts, her steely blue eyes piercing into me. A perfectly reasonable question, one might think, except her words are tinged with disdain, lingering perhaps from our brief encounter earlier.

I'm one of 35,000 people from around the world, including country presidents, activists, and employees of private sector companies, who have descended upon the desert for the United Nations Climate Conference (COP) to find collective solutions to climate change. As United Nations special advisor to end global hunger, I'm here to advocate for funding to feed millions of families impacted by climate change globally—which is what I tell her, with an irritated tone, because we both know that she knows why I'm here, having just attended my last panel discussion.

"I said, what do you think you are doing here?" she demands. For such a petite person, she has quite a gravelly, deep voice and sounds like one of those jazz singers, or a chain smoker after a pack of cigarettes.

I can't understand what Pink Hair is getting at, though I can sense a kind of smugness and enmity in her tone. Clearly, she isn't letting up. As it turns out, neither am I.

"What exactly are you getting at?" I retort.

"Don't play dumb. You know exactly what I am asking," she replies.

Actually, I don't. What I know is that I'm not about to let her subject me to a Spanish inquisition. I don't know if it's her lack of decorum or respect or a sense of entitlement, but she crawls under my skin like a bug. I gaze at her, waiting for her to go on.

"I said, *What do you think you are doing here?*" Arms crossed, she smirks at me, her demeanor telling me that she is trying to see how far she can push me, make me squirm. She glares at me silently for about thirty seconds or so.

I refuse to give her the satisfaction. "What a turnout!" I say, breaking the silence.

"What did you say?"

"I said, *What a turnout.* Isn't the number of people at this summit impressive?" A throwaway remark, perhaps, but it shifts something.

She gives a tiny, half-hearted nod as if fearful that her head might roll off her neck.

"Whatever," she shrugs. "So you think you are all that?"

I don't appreciate her tone and feel the top of my ears tingle with heat. I know I should probably turn around and walk away. It would seem to be the wisest decision in a situation like this. Pink Hair, for some reason, is intent on picking a fight. Taunting me. Challenging me. What motivates her to do so? I have no clue. Perhaps there's something about me that annoys her and rubs her the wrong way. Or perhaps this is just her vibe, so to speak. Regardless, it's becoming more evident by the second that nothing good will come from this interaction. The most mature thing is to kindly excuse myself, smile (although that seems unlikely at this stage), turn around, and walk away. The sensible part of my brain agrees.

That's not what I do. Something stops me—dignity, perhaps. Our eyes meet, and the air becomes taut and strained. That's when I realize that this is far from being over.

We stare each other down like two angry bulls inside a ring. The only thing yielding is her hair, which, having succumbed to the heat, now lays plastered across her sweaty forehead, obscuring her eyes. She raises a skinny palm to her forehead and sweeps limp hair off her face, revealing two beady brown eyes. An uneasiness hangs in the air as I carefully study her. That's when I notice it. Buried deep inside her eyes, beneath all that rage and bravado, is a kind of pain so palpable I can almost touch it. I know exactly what to do.

"Should we sit in the shade and cool down for a while?" I offer warmly, perching myself on a bench under the white canopy.

Like an immovable tree, Pink Hair stands her ground, her eyes drilling into me.

"Here, this one is for you," I offer, placing one of the two bottles I've just dug out from the bottom of my handbag beside me on the bench. I open the second bottle and guzzle tepid water down my parched throat.

Still, Pink Hair refuses to move. She doesn't venture a response. It's as though her tongue has collapsed in her mouth.

I try to understand why she is so upset. *What have I done to cause such a reaction?* As far as I know, our only interaction was in the conference room earlier. Even then, I didn't speak to her and only noticed her because of her bright pink hair, which made her stick out like a sore thumb as she sat grimacing at the back of the room. *So why is she mad at me?* I decide to get to the bottom of things; I need her to open up. So, I figure the event is an excellent topic to start with.

"Thank you so much for coming to the event. What did you think about the discussion …?"

I barely get the words out. "What did I think?" she snaps. "Are you seriously asking me that? Well, if you really want to know, I think it was a joke. I think this whole conference is a joke. I think the UN [United Nations] is a joke. There, I said it." Her right foot drives home the point, digging into the ground and unsettling dust particles.

I sit quietly, listening.

"Tell me, how does the UN justify hosting a panel discussion with no youth representation?" Her words are bitter like spoilt milk. "Don't our voices matter? You know we, too, have a lot to say about this climate crisis that you, adults, have created for us. Do you think it's fair that we work so hard and pay so much money—money we don't have, by the way—to attend these events, only to be expected to sit there quietly while UN bureaucrats lecture us about our own future?"

"No, I don't think it's fair ..."

"What do you—" her combative eyes, meeting mine, flicker with annoyance, then immediately soften. "Oh ... I see ... well, I'm glad that we at least agree on something."

Gingerly, she walks toward the bench and sits next to me. This time, she speaks quietly, as if speaking to herself. "I wish I didn't have to care about any of this. I wish I could just live my life like most of my friends. Perhaps get a job as a banker, make loads of money, and never have to worry about anyone or about the world. But sadly, I don't have that kind of luxury. This whole climate crisis thing is personal to me."

She pauses and draws a deep breath. "I was ten when my family lost everything to Hurricane Sandy in 2012. At the time, we lived on Long Island in New York. One day, we had everything: a wonderful life, a beautiful home, a loving family. And then the storm came. And just like that, we lost everything. All gone: our home, all of our belongings, everything ... gone ... reduced to a huge, useless pile of rubble. Even my dog, Daisy, died," her voice creaks.

"That's when I decided that I wanted to be a climate activist.

I knew I had to do something to be part of the solution and save humanity from ourselves. I've now been campaigning for more than a decade, and it hasn't been easy. It's hard, you know, to keep going when we keep being treated like we don't matter. When the UN doesn't seem to care about us or give us the support we need."

She uncaps the water bottle and takes a small sip.

"At the very least, they should give us a seat at the table. We want and deserve to be meaningfully engaged in all these high-level dialogues, so we can share our stories … so we can share our solutions."

As she tells me all these things, memories of my early activism come back to me in sharp focus. I remember how, earlier in my career, I was often left out of critical discussions despite possessing invaluable information that would have enabled the UN to effectively implement humanitarian programs on my African continent—simply because leadership deemed me too young. How I felt so disheartened by their disregard and was desperate for someone to give me a chance to prove my worth. The only difference is that, unlike Pink Hair, my generation was raised to ask politely and never overtly challenge elders. I admire her courage.

"Thanks so much for sharing your story, and I'm so sorry for your loss," I say, recalling the devastating impact of Hurricane Sandy.

"I shouldn't have spoken to you that way," Pink Hair softens. "I know you aren't in charge of organizing these panel discussions and that it isn't your fault. I just needed someone to listen to me—someone who can help advocate for us, that's all."

Her words sting my ears and make me kind of sad. I have met thousands of youth activists who, like Pink Hair, are working against all odds, with very few to no resources to create positive change in their communities. Their passion and steadfast hope in such uncertain times is truly admirable and embodies the spirit we need to tackle our world's enormous challenges. What if we listened more to the younger generation instead of dismissing them? Wouldn't we end up with more innovative solutions to address our challenges? What if we gave them the support and visibility they need and deserve? Wouldn't they be able to achieve so much more and help all of us accelerate change?

"If you don't mind, would it be okay if I went to your next session with you?" Pink Hair asks, yanking me out of my head, as she flashes me a warm smile.

I smile back and nod, and we get up and walk briskly toward the buildings as Pink Hair continues sharing her story with animated excitement.

This story illustrates the importance of understanding and empathy in resolving conflicts. When facing communication and intergenerational differences, it can be tempting to dismiss others, but taking the higher ground and trying to connect can lead to remarkable outcomes. By choosing not to dismiss the young activist due to her confrontational attitude and instead showing empathy, a lasting connection was formed. This not only brought personal gratification but also showcased a model of professional behavior. In our fast-paced lives, it can be challenging to manage our emotions and adjust our behavior. However, demonstrating empathy, especially when it feels undeserved, can make a significant impact, creating a space for others to feel seen and heard. This can turn potential negative outcomes into positive ones.

According to a groundbreaking study from Oxford University, our values, behaviors, and sense of self play a pivotal role in fueling intergenerational conflict in the workplace.[33] For example:

- **Values-based tensions** can arise from perceiving others through traditional versus progressive ideals. Traditionalists (often older) may be seen as resistant to change, while progressives (usually younger) may be viewed as disruptive and lacking respect for established workplace processes and procedures.
- **Behavior-based tension** often arises from attributing a colleague's actions to their generational background, such as assuming entitlement due to being Gen Z or an authoritative management style due to being a Baby Boomer.
- **Identity-based tension** occurs when we perceive sharp differences between our identity and those of others. For instance, a colleague from an older generation may value teamwork and collective effort, identifying with the "we" generation. They may see their younger colleague as part of the "me" generation, perceived as more self-serving and individualistic.

Understanding our colleagues goes beyond research. Human behavior is complex and shaped by our identities, backgrounds, beliefs, values, and experiences. We need to deeply understand others to create harmony in the workplace, rather than attributing challenges to generational differences. This involves developing human skills, such as truly listening to our colleagues, making them feel appreciated, and understanding them compassionately. In his book, *How to Know a Person*, David Brooks emphasizes this point. He says, "There is one skill that lies at the heart of any healthy person ... the ability to see someone else deeply and make them feel seen—to accurately know another person, to let them feel valued, heard, and understood."[34]

The following strategies and approaches help address key intergenerational misconceptions and challenges in the workplace.

WAYS TO MANAGE VALUE DIFFERENCES

Our generational values and desires may make it difficult for us to get along. Despite talk about generational differences in workplace preferences, a McKinsey study found that we all want similar things from work, albeit with some differences.[35] While some value an inclusive work environment over higher pay, job security over flexible schedules, or work-life balance over seniority, the research indicates that many of us share common desires in the workplace. We all want meaningful work and positive relationships with our colleagues and managers. Fair compensation and respectful treatment are universal aspirations, as is the desire to contribute meaningfully to an environment that values our perspectives. These commonalities provide a strong foundation for addressing potential intergenerational obstacles.

Invest time in finding commonalities to connect and collaborate. Consistently practicing the following daily habits will enhance interaction and understanding.

Get to Know Your Colleagues

No two people are exactly the same, including identical twins. Treating people a certain way based on their generation leads to assumptions and perpetuates stereotypes. Instead, take the time to understand your colleagues as individuals, and use this insight to build better relationships.

Maximize Contact

To improve relations and minimize intergenerational biases, it's important to engage with colleagues from different generations. Contact theory suggests that increased interaction leads to better understanding and empathy.[36] Actively seek opportunities to connect with colleagues across generations through in-person or virtual gatherings, team-building exercises, after-work activities, or showing interest in their hobbies.

Treat Others with Dignity and Respect

Regardless of our generation, we all want to be treated with dignity and respect, including younger colleagues. In the modern workplace, respect is earned. We can't expect younger colleagues to respect us simply because we are more senior; and, similarly, we can't be entitled just because we are emerging talent. We must demonstrate mutual respect to minimize intergenerational tension. If we want our colleagues to respect us, we must respect them first, even when addressing a colleague's behavior or challenging their authority.

Don't Be Ageist

Respect people of all ages and their viewpoints. Avoid using age to dismiss others' input or exclude them from important discussions. Focus on their skills, not age. When receiving advice or criticism from older colleagues, see it as an opportunity for growth, not a threat to your independence. Thank them for their feedback and evaluate their perspective with an open mind.

WAYS TO MANAGE COMMUNICATION DIFFERENCES

Navigating communication in a multigenerational workforce poses its challenges. Varied communication styles, coupled with the increasing array of communication channels and platforms, can hinder our ability to collaborate effectively. Research from Berkeley Executive Education shows that different generations prefer different communication methods (Baby Boomers and Gen Xers prefer face to face, Millennials prefer email, and Gen Z favors instant chat)—but ultimately, everyone wants to be listened to and understood.[37] Instead of trying to force our communication style on our colleagues, it's important to understand and respect their unique communication preferences. The strategies outlined next are designed to tackle the challenges of communicating across different generations.

Ask for Others' "Work Language"

Understanding colleagues' preferred communication methods is vital for productive teamwork. Take the time to discover their preferences, such as in-person conversations, phone calls, or texts. This will help reduce conflicts and boost productivity. Keep a communication cheat sheet for reference, and be willing to adapt your communication style to meet everyone's needs.

Embrace New Communication Tools

Use the latest communication tools to better connect with colleagues across different generations. Failing to do so can hurt your career and productivity. Embracing new technology will help you stay relevant and improve collaboration. It's okay to ask for help and support others in learning new tools.

Avoid Business Jargon and Slang

Communication should be clear and inclusive in a multigenerational work environment. Avoid using business jargon, such as "let's touch base with some blue sky thinking," idioms, such as "the elephant in the room," or slang, like calling your boss the GOAT, etc. as it might be confusing for others. Opt for inclusive business language to minimize communication barriers and foster workplace inclusivity.

WAYS TO MANAGE ETHICAL DIFFERENCES

We have ethical differences that make it challenging for us to collaborate. Every generation has its work ethic stereotypes. Older colleagues are seen as resistant to change and difficult to work with, while younger colleagues are considered lazy and entitled. The reality is that our attitudes and beliefs about work form these misperceptions, and our perspective often differs depending on where we stand. We might view a younger colleague as lazy for setting boundaries to achieve work-life balance while failing to realize that this is a smart decision. A Deloitte study revealed the top trait both Gen Zs and Millennials admire in their peers is having a good work-life balance, which is their main consideration when choosing a new employer.[38] We might think that older colleagues insisting on using certain workplace processes and policies are being difficult, without acknowledging that these are necessary for ethical and accountable behavior in the organization. To maintain intergenerational harmony, it's essential to respect both traditional and modern work values while allowing for flexibility. Here are some strategies to navigate work ethic across generations.

Engage in Cross-Generational Learning

Cross-generational learning can help us tap into our different experiences and perspectives at work. Older colleagues can teach younger ones how to manage their work better, while younger colleagues can help older ones build diverse networks. Mutual mentoring—pairing ourselves with a colleague from a different generation—offers valuable cross-generational insights. Senior colleagues can impart leadership skills and provide career advancement opportunities to junior ones. In turn, junior colleagues can introduce fresh perspectives and encourage senior coworkers to adaptively embrace change and technology. This exchange benefits everyone in the workplace.

Share Power

Power dynamics can lead to conflicts between generations in the workplace. Junior colleagues seek recognition, while senior colleagues want their experience to be valued. To motivate junior colleagues and boost productivity, it's important to give them opportunities to lead and share their ideas. Throughout my career, I've led successful junior teams who have proven themselves by working hard, being resourceful, and embracing new ways of thinking. As a junior team member, don't be afraid to share your perspectives and contribute to creating an inclusive workplace. Embrace your youth, and showcase your innovative thinking.

Be Flexible

Long working hours don't indicate diligence. Focus on deliverables, not the process. Younger workers prioritize work-life balance and argue that they can deliver just as much, if not more, by working smarter. Having healthy work boundaries is essential for everyone, regardless of age. Consider flexible and remote work arrangements where possible, and communicate the organization's work-life balance policy during hiring to manage expectations.

9

HOW TO ADDRESS TOKENISM

Tokenism is a prevalent issue in today's workplaces, where individuals from underrepresented groups are often brought in just to meet diversity quotas and create a façade of inclusivity. In a homogeneous work setting, being a token means being seen as a minority and not fully integrated into the majority. This damaging practice hinders real progress toward diversity and inclusion, affecting everyone negatively. To achieve genuine workplace diversity, it's crucial to proactively address tokenism and create truly inclusive environments. Those in the majority have an especially crucial role to play in ensuring that minority colleagues feel welcome and valued. While tokenism has traditionally been associated with marginalized communities, it's more complex in today's diverse work environments, as discussed in a conversation with my friend Natalie.

This chapter explores tokenism in the workplace and provides strategies to address its challenges and promote a more inclusive environment.

HUMAN SKILLS

It's October 2012 when I get an unexpected call from my friend Natalie. I haven't spoken to her for a couple of years since she relocated from New York to Mumbai, India, as part of a work transfer in her role as a principal data scientist with a big data firm based in Manhattan. As one of their top engineers, Natalie is based in India for five years to help establish the regional office.

"I've been calling for days, worried sick about you. Are you okay?" she frets.

It's lovely to hear from her under the circumstances.

"Yup, I'm alright." My voice is weary. "Sorry, the city was in a complete power blackout for days. Couldn't cook, take a hot shower, or even charge my phone," I respond, chopping vegetables to prepare my first hot meal in a week. A dust-filled beam of sunlight streams through the kitchen window.

"I know, that's insane," she exclaims. "I saw the TV coverage. Couldn't believe my eyes. A blackout in New York City, of all places!"

Hurricane Sandy had triggered massive power outages, impacting millions of people and plunging Lower Manhattan into complete darkness for almost a week.

"Anyway, thank God you're alive," she sighs. "Sorry for being MIA. I meant to get in touch, but things have been terrible at work."

She doesn't owe me an apology. We've been friends for more than a decade and have the kind of relationship that easily picks up where it left off, as is about to become evident with the call.

Her voice lowers. "I'm coming back home."

"Because of the storm? No need; everything is back to normal," I assure her.

She takes a beat as if mulling over something important, then says, "No, I'm coming home because I've thought long and hard, and it's the only solution to preserve my sanity, to stop me from having a complete mental breakdown. You know me; I don't make rash decisions."

An understatement if there was ever one. Natalie's multi-analytical personality occasionally drives me insane. She only takes calculated risks, and every decision has to be thoroughly examined, reexamined, filtered through a SWOT analysis, and reexamined again.

She goes on, "Despite my love for India, and God knows how much I love the country and the people here, my work situation has become unbearable. You know, I'm really at a breaking point."

That sounds serious. "What's happening?"

She's revved up. Ignoring my question, she trails on with her thoughts: "You know, the sad thing is that I genuinely thought I was going to make a difference, that I could finally do what I'm passionate about and help make digital spaces safer for kids and teens to navigate, given the ongoing mental health crisis. I thought they sent me halfway around the world because of my competencies, but now I realize that I was wrong. They were just using me."

"Using you?"

"Yes, can you imagine that I'm the only non-Indian staff member in an office of thirty-two?'

I keep listening.

"You know what upsets me the most is that all the signs were there from the very beginning, yet I chose to ignore them. I was just so excited about the role, determined to make things work."

"What signs?"

"A month into my job, rumors started circulating around the office that I was a token hire, only here to make our US stakeholders feel more comfortable that an American was a team leader. Or, to use their precise language, they said I was a 'transplant from HQ' to spy on the local team. The comment was so absurd that I refused to dignify it with a response. How could I be a token hire? A suburban girl from upstate New York, a token? That's insane … especially when I had all the credentials and experience required for the role."

With an engineering degree from MIT and eleven years of experience at Microsoft, I would say that if anything, Natalie was slightly overqualified for the role.

"But then I started noticing other smaller things. Like how my colleagues would often speak together in Hindi during team meetings even though the office's official language is English, which everyone speaks fluently. Or how they never included me in any social activities, because I 'wouldn't be able to get it.' Or how I kept being excluded from external stakeholder meetings despite being a team lead because I 'don't understand local customs,' which was fair, I guess. However, they also refused to help me with the onboarding process so that I could ramp up quickly and better understand cultural nuances. Eventually, I put my foot down about the external meetings with our vendors, and they obliged," she states defiantly.

"How did it go?"

"Dreadful, which is upsetting because I know that my success depends on the successful relationships that I'm able to build both internally and externally. Unfortunately, I haven't progressed much in that area, since colleagues keep trying to sabotage me."

It was a serious accusation. "How?" I ask.

"Oh, in every way possible," she was quick to respond. "Let's see ... they purposely give me the wrong protocol notes, so that I'm constantly bumbling formalities and unintentionally offending local partners. Twice, they 'accidentally' forgot to add my name to the guest list for a high-level meeting, leaving me stranded at the front desk, as I didn't have security clearance," she scoffed. "You know, these could have just been honest mistakes, but without anyone else in your corner, each and every little thing starts to add up ... like they are really out to get you."

The point has been made.

"So, you tell me, how can I continue working with people I don't trust? People who are intent on excluding me and making me fail?" she asks.

The situation is undoubtedly unsustainable. I find it difficult to respond, but I have to say something. "Have you spoken to your manager?" I suggest.

"Yes, both of them on numerous occasions. The Indian boss says I'm overly sensitive and imagining things. He says that, 'White people are too fragile and need to develop a strong backbone to cut it in India.' He says I complain too much 'for such a lady.' I mean, what does that even mean?" She sighs, and I keep listening, letting her get things off her chest.

"But that's not all," her voice wobbles. "You know, his treatment of me is just as appalling. He doesn't allow me to contribute during meetings and dismisses my recommendations. He sometimes even insists that I take notes of the meeting, saying 'as a woman,' I should 'respect the culture's hierarchical formalities.' Can you believe that?! I'm a senior engineer, for God's sake! I mean, there have been a few occasions when he did invite me to meet with key partners, but, now that I think of it, it just could have been his way of showing off our company diversity."

"And your American boss?"

"He's also part of the problem. All the support he originally promised, both in terms of resources and organizationally, vanished as soon as I arrived. And when I tried to express my concern to him, his response was flatly, 'If you can't stand the heat, get out of the kitchen.' What kind of response is that?" she sighs.

"Why didn't you say something sooner?" I add.

"To be honest with you, the situation is delicate." There's resignation in her voice. "You know, I just don't want to appear like a quitter. Also, can you imagine how it would sound—a White girl complaining about being in India? How would that come across, other than making people think I'm privileged, weak, culturally insensitive, and ungrateful?"

"But that's obviously not the case here," I jump to her defense.

"I know ... well ... I don't know," she hesitates and lets out an audible sigh. "You know, what really gets to me the most … is that you just can't treat people this way. You can't just drop someone in the middle of an unfamiliar environment with no support and leave them there to sink or swim. It's completely wrong! Without any support, anyone left to fend for themselves will most definitely sink."

I agree.

"Anyway," she carries on, "I've been thinking a lot about the past two years, just trying to make sense of everything. E, I will be damned if I let this awful work situation taint my otherwise beautiful experience in India. Having carefully analyzed the situation, I've made two significant observations."

Natalie has a natural gift for finding clarity even in the most horrendous of situations, which is one of the things I love about her. "Do tell," I inquire.

After a short silence, she continues. "First, I now know that, ultimately, the company never really intended to build the inclusive workplace here that they promised. In a way, they manipulated both me and my Indian colleagues. The only reason HQ shipped me off to India was for the optics: to appease external stakeholders, to validate with the Indian government how seriously the company was investing in India, and also, possibly, to manipulate legislatures in the US by demonstrating the company's commitment toward online child safety. My presence here was just a checking a box, a quota that needed to be filled; I'm just here as the token American."

She takes a pregnant pause. "You know, at least this has given me a new perspective. For the first time in my life, I can better relate with how some of my previous colleagues back in New York, those from marginalized groups, must have felt. I see now how difficult it must have been to be a minority in an office filled with mostly Caucasians, how dehumanizing and soul-crushing it can be to be treated like a token."

There it is: Natalie's profound introspection. I let the wisdom sink in. "How can I best support you?" I ask, words catching in my throat.

HOW TO ADDRESS TOKENISM

Working in diverse workplaces is a new experience for most of us, regardless of whether we belong to the majority or minority groups. Without active steps toward inclusion, minority group members may feel tokenized and overlooked. They may be unfairly accused of playing the "victim" card when all they want is fair treatment and acknowledgment of their value. On the other hand, those in the majority group may continue to overlook the everyday effects of tokenism —or experience frustration due to the tension caused by differences and the fear of making mistakes. For those in the majority, even with good intentions, the process can be filled with awkward and hurtful mistakes.

An illustrative example of this is when my friend Mohammed's White colleagues unintentionally excluded him from a lunch invitation because they were unsure if he would be offended by them eating non-halal meat in his presence—but were hesitant to ask. Or when my former colleague Aisha inadvertently offended two teammates by gifting Christmas presents, not realizing that they didn't observe the holiday for religious reasons. Or when that time, early in my career, with good intentions, I didn't invite any of our White colleagues to watch a film about race with my Black colleagues, as I didn't want to make them feel uncomfortable. Or when the zealous intern in my previous company petitioned for an all-gender bathroom, only to end up unintentionally outing a colleague's private sexual identity. Or when my friend Mark in Silicon Valley asked female candidates to interview in a bar, thinking it was a gesture of equal treatment to how he interviewed male candidates.

These examples clearly demonstrate that navigating diversity is a significant challenge without possessing strong human skills and cultural competencies.

The following strategies provide ways to combat tokenism.

HUMAN SKILLS

WAYS TO AVOID LEADERSHIP "TOKENISM"

The team lacks diversity in leadership, with only one minority holding a prominent role. This individual feels isolated and unsupported by those in the majority.

Majority Solution: True workplace diversity goes beyond token hires. Update exclusionary policies, and focus on increasing representation at all levels. As part of the majority, you must proactively bridge gaps and ensure everyone feels fully integrated as a team member. Actively seek opportunities for minority leaders to share their unique perspectives and make meaningful contributions. This could mean inviting them to key meetings or seeking their input on important projects. Appreciate them in their entirety, recognizing their humanity, talents, and experiences. With the increasingly global nature of work, it's essential to treat others with the same respect and inclusivity that we would hope for ourselves. At an event in New Jersey, Tony, a pharmaceutical executive, shared his perspective:

> *A few years ago, my biases almost led to a major mistake while leading a project for a new medication. We were behind schedule when our CEO hired a chief diversity officer. This led to unconscious bias training and distractions, causing missed deadlines and product formula problems. After a heated meeting with the CEO, the chief diversity officer came to my office. I felt annoyed to see her and blamed her for my situation. To my surprise, she claimed to have a solution to the product's problem. I initially doubted her expertise, but after reviewing her notes with my scientists, it turns out she had a PhD in chemistry and had worked as a pharmacist. I realized I should have consulted her sooner. Now, I make sure*

to thoroughly review all new hires' resumes and learn about their experiences before making judgments.

Minority Solution: Remember, you are a leader in this team. Use your position to advocate for more diversity and inclusion. One person may be a token, two may be a minority, but three or more can truly make a difference and have a voice.

Are you tired of feeling unheard? Team up with like-minded colleagues, and seek support from the majority group to ensure your concerns are taken seriously and not dismissed as a "minority issue."

Kerry, a female executive at a tech company, found herself as one of only two females among seven leaders, with the rest being male. The other male executives would spend their weekends playing golf with the CEO, where major decisions were made. Kerry, with no interest in golf and family commitments on weekends, voiced her concern to the CEO, who promised she would be included in critical decisions. The situation didn't improve, so she reluctantly decided to take golfing classes and join the weekend gatherings to ensure her contributions were not sidelined.

One evening, during a clubhouse gathering, she discovered that two of her male colleagues also disliked golf and only played to please the CEO. They bonded over the struggle to balance work and family obligations. Along with the other female leader, the group of four successfully demanded that major decisions be brought to the team for a majority vote, leading to a better work-life balance for all. "That's not to say that all decision-making outside the office has ceased, as the CEO still indulges in golf with the other two male leaders," Kerry told me. "However, now, he can't unilaterally approve major decisions without a majority vote, forcing him to bring all key issues to our team meetings." She paused, reflecting, "It's a relief to finally have a semblance of work-life balance, and I know I couldn't have achieved this on my own."

WAYS TO AVOID "TOKEN" PROMOTIONS

We have promoted a minority team member, so why do they feel the need to ask for extra compensation or authority? Shouldn't the promotion and increased visibility be enough?

Majority Solution: It's unfair to put a minority staff member in a leadership position without giving them sufficient authority. Remember, in a hierarchical organization, titles and levels of authority are critical as they show who is responsible for key decisions and how much they can be trusted. Without the necessary authority, their credibility and effectiveness are undermined. If you want them to succeed, make sure they have the same level of authority as other team members in similar positions. Failing to do so will devalue them and may lead to their departure.

The insightful CEO of a top-tier media company, Lauren, confided in me during our meeting in Manhattan:

> *I mistreated my former chief of staff by taking her for granted and not supporting her promotion to a role she was qualified for because I couldn't bear the thought of losing her. She was one of just two Hispanic women on the team, and I knew her leaving would hinder my diversity goals. I thought a salary raise would make up for the missed opportunity, but she resigned a few months later. I always saw myself as her mentor, but I messed it all up. My advice: Appreciate your staff and recognize and reward their efforts. Encourage and celebrate their achievements, and don't hold them back from progressing in their careers. I know it's easier said than done.*

HOW TO ADDRESS TOKENISM

Minority Solution: Make sure you set the standard for how you deserve to be treated. Don't let your boss undervalue you or exploit your skills. If you're offered a promotion, watch out for signs of it being fake. If the new title comes with more responsibilities, make sure you have a conversation with your boss or HR to negotiate fair compensation. Research similar job titles using platforms such as LinkedIn or Glassdoor. Consider your location and the cost of living to support your request.

Know your priorities when negotiating. Consider whether you prefer authority and influence over a higher salary. Could you use influence to get a higher salary later? Or is it better to focus on getting a higher salary now and building influence later? Determine what's most important for your long-term career satisfaction.

When negotiating explore all benefits, such as equity or additional leave days. Carefully weigh your options, and choose what's best for you. If negotiations fail, consider staying in your current role or transitioning to another department. Advocate for yourself, and don't settle for an environment where your contributions aren't appreciated. Leverage the offer of a promotion to enhance your professional profile, and actively pursue new opportunities elsewhere.

On a recent visit to Toronto, Canada, Felix, an HR specialist at an engineering company, shared this valuable insight with me:

> *When I started at the company, I struggled to advocate for myself in a female-dominated HR department. I felt overlooked for promotions by my female boss. The company aimed for a gender-balanced executive team, but we couldn't fill the roles. I suggested revising the job descriptions to eliminate gender-biased language, which seemed overly geared towards a masculine perspective—as I believed this was a factor in the lack of female applicants for the positions. The plan was a success. We observed an increase in the number of female*

candidates for leadership roles, and we successfully appointed them, achieving gender parity within the executive team. I felt proud of my contribution. By taking initiative and demonstrating leadership, I gained my manager's trust and was rewarded with a well-deserved promotion.

WAYS TO AVOID DISMISSING VALUABLE INPUT

We have included a diverse team member in our meeting, so why do they rarely speak up, and why do they believe their input is not being valued when they do?

Majority Solution: Inviting a minority colleague to meetings is a good start, but genuine inclusion means valuing and considering their input. Remember, teams only gain a competitive edge if the diverse team members feel valued and their unique perspective is truly considered. Research shows minority voices are often marginalized, so we must actively encourage their participation. If the team member isn't contributing, it may indicate they don't feel included. Thus, focus on building trust, and offer constructive feedback to help them grow. Where possible, consider inviting other qualified minority colleagues to ensure that your minority colleague doesn't feel isolated. Remember that an inclusive meeting ensures everyone can freely express thoughts and ideas. Dismissing minority perspectives not only lowers team performance, it perpetuates harmful notions and undermines their dignity. As author and psychologist Adam Grant shared, "… you won't understand the views of a group until you've invited the quieter voices into the discussion."[39]

Make it a priority to ensure that all voices are heard in meetings, especially those of your minority colleagues. Set the stage at the beginning of the meeting by expressing genuine interest in hearing diverse perspectives. Implement a speaking time limit to give everyone an equal opportunity to share their thoughts. Proactively encourage contributions from minority colleagues without singling them out, and provide alternative channels for communication, such as email or collaboration tools like Slack. For instance, you can say, "These are all brilliant ideas, but I wonder if I'm missing something." Your efforts in fostering an inclusive environment will lead to more valuable discussion

Chip, the COO of a start-up mobile games publisher in Los Angeles, shared a story with me about feeling like a fish out of water after transitioning from being part of the majority to suddenly becoming a minority. He mentioned how a considerate act during a meeting from a member of the majority made a significant impact, ultimately saving a crucial business deal:

> *When our small gaming company was being acquired by a French company two years ago, I traveled back and forth to Paris to negotiate the terms of the deal. I realized I was in over my head when everyone in the meeting started speaking French. I didn't want to come across as arrogant by insisting they speak English, so one of the executives provided me with simultaneous translations. It was quite an experience to find myself as a minority in an all-White environment.*

Minority Solution: Understand why your input is being overlooked, and take accountability. If your contributions need improvement, focus on enhancing your skills to make a more significant impact. If colleagues are tokenizing your presence, consider not attending those meetings. Being consistently ignored can diminish your confidence. If company policy mandates minority representation, your colleagues will be compelled to invite other minorities. Introducing other individuals from minority groups will humanize everyone and promote fair treatment. If minority colleagues share similar concerns, it reveals a blind spot in the organization that needs addressing.

It's important to provide opportunities for other minorities to participate in crucial meetings. Constantly being singled out to "represent" our community is unfair and may lead to rejection from our own group, risking exclusion by both sides.

At an activist rally in Los Angeles, Jing, an employee at a major cosmetic company, stressed the significance of engaging members of our community in our efforts:

> *I was the only Asian person being invited to the planning meetings for a corporate social responsibility program in response to the "Stop Asian Hate" campaign. The PR department had already put together a publicity package without speaking to me or any of my Asian colleagues. When I raised concerns, the PR director silenced me, saying it was too late to make changes. I realized management was using me as their scapegoat. I recommended that my Asian colleague attend the meetings instead, and soon there were three of us with similar concerns. We drafted an email with our joint input and sent it to management, which finally made them listen. This process spared me from coming across as the office gossip, as my Asian colleagues were able to witness for themselves what was happening behind closed doors.*

WAYS TO AVOID "TOKENISTIC" REPRESENTATION

We're proud of our minority hire, so why shouldn't we showcase their image to highlight the company's inclusivity and honor them?

Majority Solution: It's important to avoid tokenism in diversity efforts. Using a minority colleague as the sole representation of diversity without meaningful inclusion in decision-making processes is disingenuous and can harm the company's reputation. Instead, focus on attracting and hiring more diverse candidates. Also, remember that not everyone enjoys having their image used, and doing so repeatedly can make them feel tokenized. When involving minority colleagues in public engagements, let's ensure their involvement is meaningful, enabling them to showcase their work, knowledge, and expertise.

My friend Alice, a British speechwriter with a postgraduate degree in linguistics, was thrilled to be offered a job with a telecommunications company in South Africa. Her excitement turned to disappointment when she realized that the company was primarily interested in using her connections to facilitate the launch of their products in the UK, rather than her expertise. Frustrated, she expressed this:

> *I realized after six months at the company that I was hired as a strategic tool to lure British investors. My main job was to write the CEO's speeches and messages for the media, but he never used any of my work. Instead, he would showcase me in meetings with Western investors, using my presence as a symbol of trust, saying things like, "Your investments are secure with us, as we have one of your own on our team." It felt like I was being treated as a commodity rather than a respected team member.*

Minority Solution: You have the right to request that your image not be used for company propaganda, even if it benefits you personally. If you become your company's face of diversity or inclusion, negotiate some influence over diversity and inclusion efforts. If you're not successful, use your public profile to find other opportunities, like Sacha did.

I met Sacha on the subway in New York. She shared her experience of giving up on trying to improve her situation at the car manufacturing company where she worked as senior vice president (SVP) of diversity.

HUMAN SKILLS

Despite the initial fanfare about her joining the company, Sacha found herself with a limited budget and little influence. Frustrated with the lack of progress, she shifted her focus to raising her profile externally by engaging with the media, writing for publications, and attending high-level conferences and events. This led to her being offered a new position with better prospects elsewhere.

WAYS TO DEAL WITH AUTHENTICITY CHALLENGES

We pride ourselves on being an inclusive culture, yet our minority hires have expressed they do not feel they can be their authentic selves at work. What does that even mean?

Majority Solution: What may not be obvious if we're part of the majority group is that many minority colleagues feel the need to dilute their authentic selves to fit into the mainstream, known as *masking*. This involves concealing who they are to assimilate or reduce discrimination. For example, a Black female colleague might hide their natural hair under a wig to conform to "beauty standards," while a female executive might suppress her empathy to avoid being seen as too emotional. Similarly, a male colleague might hide his personal struggles to avoid being perceived as insensitive to the struggles of others, and a transgender colleague might dress conservatively to fit in.

The act of masking extends to various facets of diversity, with individuals concealing their disability, regional accent, or transgender identity to sidestep potential bias and secure opportunities. This behavior can take a toll on employees, impacting their mental well-being and diminishing their ability to fully contribute to the workplace. The majority of people, including those in leadership positions, feel pressure to mask their true selves at work. A 2023 Deloitte study found that 60 percent of US workers have concealed their true selves at work in the past year. This included 66 percent of Asian individuals, 68 percent of Black individuals, 62 percent of Hispanic individuals, 56 percent of White individuals, 69 percent of non-heterosexual individuals, and 71 percent of individuals with disabilities or long-term physical illnesses. This has significant negative effects on overall health, with 60 percent of workers reporting adverse impacts on their well-being.[40]

Jess, a sports executive, shared his experience with me in Brooklyn:

> *I spent a significant portion of my career hiding my queer identity from my all-male team. I felt pressured to fit into a "bro" culture and keep my love for RuPaul's Drag Race a secret. When I accidentally ran into my boss wearing a pink tutu and heels, I decided to embrace my true self. Unfortunately, my boss distanced himself from me, so I left and joined a new company where I could be myself from day one. I decided that I was tired of hiding who I am.*

We all have the right to bring our authentic selves to the workplace. Our individual stories and perspectives should be embraced and celebrated. When we conceal parts of who we are, we create barriers that hinder genuine connections and trust. Masking our true identities can lead to feelings of inadequacy, unworthiness, and shame.

Take the time to understand and embrace your colleagues' unique expression. Unless their actions breach company guidelines, they should have the same freedom to express themselves as anyone else. Their identity and background can offer fresh perspectives, drive innovation, and lead to greater success.

Be mindful of how your words and actions can impact minority colleagues. Avoid stereotypes and treat people as individuals. Don't ask invasive questions or make remarks based on race. Approach questions with tact and respect. Creating a genuine relationship beyond work can be valuable. Finding common ground through shared interests can foster understanding, creating a safe and inclusive environment for all.

HUMAN SKILLS

Minority Solution: Most companies won't become inclusive overnight, but your work environment should allow you to be yourself and feel safe, embracing all aspects of your personality, including your unique quirks. It should value your experiences and perspectives.

Stand up against colleagues asking you to perform clichéd acts such as "walking gay" or "sounding sassy." Your identity and culture are not entertainment. Set your boundaries and speak out.

Being authentic means being true to ourselves while maintaining professionalism. We should be mindful of our actions and refrain from sharing intimate details, using inappropriate language, or dressing casually unless the job calls for it.

To foster understanding and empathy among colleagues, celebrate your unique identity, and connect with them through official National "X" days. The more familiar someone seems, the more comfortable we feel around them.

During our catch-up call, my friend José, who works for a printing company in South Carolina, expressed the value of this approach:

> My colleagues and I organized a potluck for our end-of-year holiday party as a cost-saving measure. I prepared chiles en nogada using my grandmother's recipe, and everyone brought their own traditional home-cooked meals. The event was a great success, with people sharing stories about their cultures and enjoying the food and dancing. It was eye-opening to see how much we all have in common, regardless of cultural background. The CEO mentioned that he learned more about our cultures in one evening than in all his unconscious bias training. I believe the event changed the way my colleagues see the Mexican culture for the better, and we can do it again.

10

HOW TO BE AN ALLY

The significance of allyship cannot be emphasized enough. It is an essential pillar in creating a truly fair and inclusive workplace. Allyship demands active support for our colleagues in their quest for equality, especially in diverse environments where individuals have differing levels of privilege. While the link between allyship and privilege has historically made some uncomfortable, we must embrace this discomfort and strive for positive change. Today's workplace offers us a significant opportunity to redefine allyship, challenging traditional power dynamics and fostering a more equal and just work environment.

Gone are the days when allyship meant the majority supporting minorities. Now, minorities have the power to stand together and be allies, empowering each other and advocating for change. They can also become allies to the majority, showing them how to address the needs of their minority communities. These alliances can be mutually beneficial and help ensure that everyone is actively engaged. It's important to acknowledge that some allies may need to see how these efforts benefit them personally or their immediate environment. Tapping into these motivations can be a powerful force for positive change, as this story about Leo, an ally for gender equality, exemplifies. It is followed by effective strategies for allyship.

"I just don't get it. What's up with women? What is it that you actually want?" Leo asks me as soon as we finish exchanging pleasantries.

I am taken by surprise. I leisurely sip my sparkling water and wait for details. It's spring 2023, and we're at the illustrious Carnegie Hall in Midtown Manhattan, chatting over exquisite cocktails. Tonight, I am set to address a distinguished audience of eighty-five chief information officers from Fortune 500 companies, including industry giants such as Nike, Microsoft, Apple, IBM, Boeing, HP, and more. My focus will be on guiding them towards fostering inclusive workplaces.

Among the attendees is Leo, who's inquiry has grabbed my attention. Standing next to him is an elegantly-attired brunette, roughly five foot six, in her early fifties. She exudes sophistication in a sleeveless black shift dress, strappy silver sandals, and a timeless pearl necklace. Her oval face is framed by tousled, shoulder-length hair, and her captivating brown eyes are accentuated by trendy, green-rimmed circular glasses.

"Eh, this should be fun," the brunette remarks sarcastically, flashing me a warm smile, and quickly glancing sideways toward a giant floor-to-ceiling window, as if to say, *Let's make a run for it.* Her voice is comforting, like a cup of warm milk with honey.

She leans over and says, "Hi, I'm____," but the classical music playing in the background swallows her name.

"Seriously, what do women want?" Leo presses on with his inquisition. He awkwardly swirls his glass, spilling red wine down his hairy arm, which he ignores.

"You know what I really don't get? One minute, women say they want men to support advancing gender equality, yet when we engage, they can't stop criticizing everything we say or do." He gives me a significant look and shrugs.

I know Leo, but not well enough to decipher his loaded message. We met several years ago when his company, a leading tech firm, invited me to give a keynote address on the importance of male allyship in the workplace. Since then, we've seen each other a handful of times to brainstorm how to address inclusion implementation challenges in the corporate world. Leo is usually upbeat, but not tonight—tonight, his soul seems burdened.

"What's going on?" I ask, taking in his lanky frame—*late forties, roughly six feet tall* —slender face, strong jaw, blue eyes, and mop of curly, blond hair. He wears a beige pair of crisply-ironed chino pants, a pale-blue shirt with rolled-up sleeves, and black leather penny loafers.

"I've been having major issues with the two senior female executives who cochair our company's women's network, and it's all become a huge headache," he sighs. "You see, last year, they asked me to launch an internal male allyship program as an extension of the women's network. I was really honored to be asked, so I immediately said yes. I even got most of our male senior leaders to sign up, which wasn't a small feat. But we did it, and we got off to a great start."

Good for Leo. Male allyship enables men to share the burden of ending workplace discrimination, letting them be positive role models among their peers by championing equality. It can accelerate progress toward more equity, as men still occupy more positions of influence and power than women in the corporate world. Research from the John Hopkins Carey Business School shows that men can support women's aspirations without fear of being perceived as acting in self-interest; they can challenge other men for their biased behavior or sexist language without penalty; and their engagement has the knock-on effect of giving women more confidence to confront inequality.[41]

"So what happened?" I ask, intrigued.

"Before long, the cochairs invited me and some of the guys to sit on gender panels at key internal and external events. Everything seemed to be going well until, all of a sudden, it wasn't. We started having major problems." Like a dark cloud on a sunny day, a veil of gloom dims the light in Leo's eyes.

"What kind of problems?" the brunette amiably asks, seeing he was genuinely looking for help. When Leo responds, I learn that her name is Margaret.

"Some women started complaining about our participation on the gender panels. They accused us of hijacking the women's agenda and taking the spotlight away from them. They said we were using the network to look good and self-promote. It was totally unexpected and caught us off guard, given we were there at their invitation. Anyway, things came to a head two months ago, and the situation has now gone from bad to worse."

"What happened?" I inquire.

"To mark Women's History Month, a few of the guys proposed that we advocate for a paid parental leave policy to give any new parent time off. But we were immediately met with pushback and were told that the women were only interested in pushing for more maternity leave. That's when things began to deteriorate, and the attacks intensified. We were accused of making everything about men and promoting, I quote, 'yet another scheme to give men more benefits at the expense of women,' which was completely not the case. We thought parental leave was a great way to show true allyship, allowing men and other genders to share the burden of care work and parenting, because we recognized that women have traditionally had to sacrifice their careers to be the primary caregivers. But no matter how much we tried to reason with the cochairs, they shut us down and claimed they felt controlled."

Leo is right. Parental leave is nondiscriminatory in that it benefits all parents regardless of gender or whether they gave birth or adopted—and therefore is more inclusive. Research, including from Harvard Business Review, shows that in many companies offering maternity leave, women are often reluctant to take the time off, fearing it will damage their careers.[42] In contrast, when male senior leaders partake in parental leave, they challenge caregiver stereotypes and stigmas and minimize women's fears of taking time off.

That said, I immediately spot two problems with Leo's plans. First, opponents of paid parental leave worry that it leads to discrimination against women by not factoring in the extra time needed for women to heal post-birth—so the pushback is totally understandable. Second, the timing of trying to launch a male-led initiative during the one month in the year dedicated to celebrating women is also a problem.

I share my thoughts with Leo: "The first thing to remember is that allyship comes with many expectations. In this case, your female colleagues want to see a true commitment from men to address their issues. Consultation is key, and so is listening. No one is looking for a savior to swoop in, take over, and try to fix things. Instead, they need true partnership. Women have been dealing with gender inequality all their lives; they know the challenges and what needs to be done to make things equal—making them great leaders in helping build more inclusive workplaces. In order for that to happen, they must lead the process of identifying challenges and priority issues to champion. They must set the agenda for you, as allies, to support."

I pause and check in with Leo. He intently nods, and I continue, "Regarding the parental leave policy, I think it's a brilliant plan and something the company should pursue down the line in consultation with the women's network and all other employee networks. That's what great allyship should be—support for others in the way they wish to be supported, instead of setting your own agenda."

"I realize that now. It's rather unfortunate, because we really never meant to offend anyone. We were just trying to support. I guess we just jumped into our usual lets-fix-it male mode, instead of allowing them to lead."

"Intent versus impact," I respond.

"Exactly. But the biggest issue for us guys wasn't the actual pushback; it's that all our attempts to have a meaningful conversation were shut down. To be accused of being 'controlling' in this post-#MeToo area is very damaging, especially when all we were trying to do was to explain our intent, realign, and hopefully move the proposal forward. The attacks were so unfair and made our whole engagement with the network feel disingenuous."

"Disingenuous, how exactly?" Margaret asks.

"Well, there was certainly a big disconnect between the ideals of feminism and how some of these feminists behaved toward men. I have worked hard to become more informed and now even consider myself a feminist because I now know that it simply means I believe in gender equality, but it didn't seem like they cared about true equality. We thought we were going to discuss our challenges and unify around a common goal of liberating all genders. Instead, we were expected to show up to the monthly meetings and sit in silence while women lectured us about our 'evil' ways. We wouldn't be allowed to interject, challenge things, or even share any of our thoughts and ideas." His tone is calm, but he is clearly irritated—even though he tries to hide it from us.

"This may be hard for you to hear, Leo," Margaret challenges, "but this has been the female experience from the very beginning of time: show up, look pretty, be polite, don't say a word, don't challenge men, don't disagree, don't show that you have thoughts of your own. Finally, after being silenced or ignored for so long, our voices are being heard. We are finally saying, 'Hear us, see our pain, understand our struggles, and show us that you care.' Surely men can understand that? I—"

"I can't speak for other men," Leo cut in, "but I personally have no issues with women advocating for themselves; in fact, I support them. I do, however, have two glaring issues with some aspects of feminism. One, I have a problem with men being blamed for all of the ills experienced by women, or with the notion that we are all evil.

I think that some of you feminists think that men walk around all day thinking about ways to oppress women, when the truth is most guys don't even have enough time to think about their own well-being, let alone women's. We are busy breaking our backs, trying to put food on the table to pay bills, to send our kids to school. We—"

"But Leo, that…?"

"Please Margaret, let me finish?" Flustered, Leo wipes his brow and stutters over his words, "Se-se-second. We are sick and tired of being sold a lie. We are—"

"What lie?" Margaret interjects.

"The lie that if we all sign up for feminism and put in the hard work, that there will be some payoff. Frankly, most guys aren't buying it anymore. We have yet to see the proof. In my case, working with the women's network only further cemented my doubts. Apparently, we can't acknowledge male suffering, because it diminishes women's experiences. I just don't buy that. I think there is enough room in this world for all our emotions. I think—"

"But Leo, you're missing the point," Margaret sighs quietly. "Sadly, at this current time, it does take away the spotlight from women's issues. As I said before, we are finally at a time when women's issues are being pushed to the fore. We live in a world of scarcity and hyperactivity where resources are limited, and people's attention spans are short. We have to be mindful not to drown out the few courageous females whose voices have begun to surface. We also have to strategically use limited resources to fund initiatives that can equalize things for women and allow them to at least catch up to where most men are."

"Sorry to belabor the point, but what I'm trying to say is equally important, and I don't think that you are getting me," Leo says, lowering his voice and choosing his words carefully. "Let me start by saying that I hear you and agree that we must level the playing field for women, which is why I've been trying to play my part. But at the same time, I must insist that we can't dismiss the experiences of men and then expect them to be a hundred percent committed to a movement that either openly villainizes them or constantly questions their motives."

He sips his wine and clears his throat. "If retribution is all that women want—to make us all feel the pain that you all feel, to make us walk around with our heads hanging in shame—then please go right ahead, keep doing what you're doing. Keep attacking us, and let's see how far that gets us. However, if you want to make real change, there is a better and more inclusive way to achieve this—and we are here for it. So instead of silencing male allies, engage us and let us give you the inside scoop directly from the horse's mouth on how to engage other men and make them care about gender equality. Because when you invite male allies to your meetings and silence them, it's the equivalent of a doctor who learns they are chronically ill, gathers all the best specialists, and then asks everyone to sit and watch as they issue their own diagnosis while refusing any other input or suggestions. After a while, the other specialists will look at each other, question why they are even there, decide they are wasting their time, and leave. This is what's happening with some of the guys in the allyship initiative; they are questioning what's in it for them, and many are dropping out."

"But that's a huge problem right there. You can't enter an allyship dialogue with a 'what's-in-it-for-me?' attitude," Margaret challenges.

"Why not?" Leo objects.

As they continue their lively debate, I find myself pondering the essence of true allyship: empathy. Genuine allyship requires us to stop tearing each other down based on our differences. It's natural to reciprocate dislike, so we can't expect men to advocate for gender equality if they feel attacked. Similarly, women have every right to raise their voices against mistreatment. It's unjust to demonize all men or belittle women and minorities fighting for their rights. These reflections stay with me as I express gratitude to Leo for sharing his story and head towards the stage.

The story above powerfully illustrates the difficulties of discussing allyship, highlighting how these conversations can become deeply personal and trigger defensiveness. This barrier frequently dissuades people from embracing allyship, impeding our collective progress. Nevertheless, within our diverse professional landscapes, there exists an opportunity to embrace a fresh approach to mutual allyship, enabling us to consistently learn from each other and reduce the fear of making missteps.

For example, a male colleague can serve as an ally to a female colleague to promote gender equality. Similarly, she can be an ally to a colleague from the LGBTQI community to advocate for gay rights, who in turn can support a Black colleague in their efforts to advance racial equity, and so on. Mutual allyship also extends to minority groups. For instance, White, Black, and Hispanic female colleagues can be allies in striving for pay equity—as a vast gulf still separates the earnings of Black and Hispanic women from the earnings of White men. (According to Pew Research Center, in 2022, White women earned 83 percent as much as White men, compared to Black women, who earned 70 percent, and Hispanic women, who earned only 65 percent as much).[43]

In addition, a notable aspect of the modern workplace is the constant evolution and challenge of our privileges, particularly when collaborating within global teams. For instance, a White colleague who hadn't previously considered the impact of race might suddenly find themselves in the minority after transitioning from headquarters to a regional office. Similarly, a female executive could encounter gender discrimination when her decision-making authority diminishes upon being promoted to a male-dominated C-suite.

HUMAN SKILLS

WAYS TO BE AN ALLY

Embracing these new changes and opportunities will help form powerful allyships, fostering personal and professional growth while broadening our perspectives. To become an impactful ally, consider the following strategies.

Listen and Show Empathy

To truly become an ally, we must start by actively listening to our colleagues and making a genuine effort to understand their experiences and perspectives. It's crucial to recognize that the responsibility of learning and awareness lies with us. We can accelerate our progress by reading, listening, or watching relevant content. Approaching conversations with humility and a learning mindset is essential to becoming a great ally. By doing so, our colleagues feel supported in their journey and respected. Remember, always seek permission before delving into personal matters during conversations. For instance, you could say:

- "Can you shed light on the daily challenges women encounter in this organization that might not be immediately apparent to me?"
- "In your opinion, what is the most impactful action that our White colleagues could take to enhance the working environment for people of color?"
- "What specific steps can I take to demonstrate my commitment to being an ally for you?"

The more we educate ourselves about the struggles of others, the better equipped we are to show empathy. Allyship also demands that we are open to unlearning language and concepts that contribute to exclusion. This means refraining from using discriminatory language, such as saying "tone-deaf" to convey a lack of understanding, which excludes those with hearing disabilities. We must also avoid making assumptions about a colleague's sexual orientation or gender identity by asking about their spouse instead of their partner. We must resist the urge to assume we comprehend someone's beliefs or religion and instead engage in respectful conversations to gain understanding.

Be a Supporter, Not a Savior

Allyship isn't about "saving" our colleagues or imposing our support on them. It's about supporting them in ways that they want to be supported. While it may be tempting to jump to their defense when they are unfairly treated, please refrain from doing so. This can undermine their ability to stand up for themselves and may harm their self-esteem. One study revealed that Black students who received unsolicited help from White peers reported lower self-esteem about their own competence than Black students who did not receive assumptive help.[44] Instead, take the time to find the right moment outside of the situation to ask what kind of support they might require from you in future situations.

Remember, allyship is not a one-size-fits-all concept. Not all minorities need your help. Equally, different people within the same minority group have different experiences and needs. For example, a colleague may welcome your help in correcting others who misgender them, or they may prefer to handle it themselves. Always ask if your support is wanted. If not, respect that and don't insist on helping. Unwanted support can be intrusive.

Remember, being an ally is more than just a title. It requires ongoing dedication to advocating for those in need. Don't seek allyship for personal validation or praise, or to feel superior to others.

If you are the person in need of support, remember that you can't force someone into becoming an ally or use their privileges against them. Not everyone will share your passion for an issue, and that's okay. Unless it's mandated by company policy, your colleague has the right to decide not to support your cause, just as you have the right to advocate for it.

Stay Curious, Not Perfect

Allyship is complex in that the appropriate approach in one scenario might not apply in another, as individuals, even within the same group, may have varied needs and expectations. Therefore, it's natural to make mistakes despite our best efforts. By acknowledging our shortcomings and being open about them, we can navigate these challenges more effectively. For example, expressing vulnerability by admitting, "I'm actively educating myself, but I may not always get it right. I'm eager to learn, so I hope you can guide me when I make mistakes," displays sincerity and a willingness to grow.

Furthermore, equipping ourselves with the necessary skills can help us anticipate and address potential conflicts. The "Boots and Sandals" exercise, developed by productivity coach Presley Pizzo,[45] offers valuable insights into how our words and actions as allies may inadvertently cause harm. This exercise serves as a powerful tool for fostering understanding and promoting responsible allyship.

The Boots and Sandals Exercise

Imagine that having certain privileges in life is like wearing a well-made and comfortable pair of heavy boots that protect against all the elements and harm. Now imagine you accidentally step on the toes of your colleague, who happens to be wearing a pair of open sandals. Because your boots are so heavy, you don't realize what you have done until your colleague screams, "Ouch, you're hurting *me*." How do you respond? We know that the appropriate way to de-escalate the situation is to immediately remove our foot and apologize; however, when it comes to allyship, most people get defensive, turning an otherwise innocent accident into a hugely divisive issue. A problematic response is often along the following lines.

- **Making it about ourselves:** "How dare you accuse me of hurting you when I'm such a great person?!"

- **Denying others of their experience:** "What's the big deal? I don't mind having people stepping on my toes."
- **Deflecting:** "I can't believe you're making such a big deal about your toes when others don't even have toes. That's what we should be talking about."
- **Refusing to acknowledge the impact:** "All toes matter!"
- **Policing their tone:** "You know what? I would move my foot if you asked me nicely."
- **Refusing to admit that there is a solution:** "You must understand that toes get stepped on daily. The sooner you accept this reality, the better it is for you."
- **Blaming the victim:** "It's your fault. What were you even doing walking around people wearing boots? You ought to be more careful."
- **Withdrawing our support:** "I thought you needed my help. That's it. I'm done helping."

It's evident that these responses are absurd and unhelpful. By taking accountability for our actions in the moment, an ally can proactively minimize making a mistake.

- **Step 1:** Stop the hurt by immediately removing your foot. If you are speaking, stop talking and listen to your colleague.
- **Step 2:** Acknowledge the impact and check in. For example, ask, "Are you okay?"
- **Step 3:** Listen to your colleague's response and learn.
- **Step 4:** Apologize, even if the harm wasn't intentional. For example, say, "I'm sorry; I wasn't paying attention. I didn't mean to cause harm."
- **Step 5:** Stop the pattern by being mindful of your words next time or where you place your foot. This may require that you change your footwear to minimize harm to others.

WAYS TO ADDRESS AN OFFENSE

When you inadvertently offend a colleague, it's crucial to hold yourself accountable. Rather than dismissing or avoiding the issue, take their feedback seriously, and take ownership of your actions by offering a sincere apology. Avoid the temptation to argue or persuade them to see your perspective. Instead, focus on acknowledging the mistake and making things right.

Apologize Without Being Defensive

An effective apology comes from the heart and reflects genuine humility. It's not about putting on a show or boosting our own ego. Instead, it's about validating the other person's feelings and owning up to our mistakes. A sincere apology also involves outlining concrete steps to make amends and prevent a repeat of the same errors in the future.

When uncertain, it's important to approach your colleague with humility and seek their guidance. You might say something like, "I truly want to make amends and would appreciate your input on how best to proceed." Follow this by presenting your initial ideas, demonstrating your dedication to resolving the issue.

Respect Boundaries and Emotions

When offering an apology, it's essential to respect your colleague's boundaries and choose the right time and approach. Start by respectfully acknowledging the need for an apology: "I would like to apologize for my words and actions and wondered if now is a good time." Pay attention to their cues and guidance. They might need time to process their emotions before they're ready to receive your apology, or they may prefer to express their feelings before hearing your words.

It's counterproductive to apologize when your emotions are running high or you're feeling upset, as this can exacerbate the situation. Don't hesitate to request some time for self-reflection and to gather your thoughts and emotions before delivering a heartfelt apology.

Keep in mind that even the sincerest apology may not always resolve everything or be embraced. It's possible that your colleague may choose not to forgive you or to cut off contact altogether. Though it may be difficult, we cannot force someone to forgive us. What we can do is honor their choice and focus on moving forward. Taking ownership of our mistakes and recognizing that we have apologized allows us to uphold our integrity and seek closure. If you are fortunate enough to receive forgiveness, take the time to deeply reflect on your actions and make a sincere promise to strive for betterment.

Be Gracious

When receiving an apology, be gracious. In allyship, it's crucial to recognize that understanding and compassion should flow in both directions. If you receive an apology, it's important to refrain from publicly shaming others for their mistakes. While they may not get everything right, it's essential not to dismiss everything—they are on a journey, and it's important to give them the chance to learn and evolve. Expressing gratitude can make a significant impact, as can reflecting on and taking responsibility for our role in any misunderstandings.

WAYS TO MINIMIZE MICROAGGRESSIONS

Is your colleague truly overly sensitive, or could it be that your own biases are clouding your perception of them? Perhaps your actions unintentionally contribute to their sensitivity. It's important to recognize that even well-meaning individuals may hold biases that manifest as microaggressions toward others. These microaggressions can make others feel invalidated or attacked based on their marginalized identities, such as race, gender, sexual orientation, disability, religion, or class, regardless of our intentions. For instance:

- **A racial microaggression** could be excluding a Black colleague from team projects, conveying the message that they are insignificant, or telling a Hispanic American colleague that they are eloquent in English, implying that they are not true Americans.
- **A gender microaggression** could be an assertive female being called "bossy" while a confident male boss is called a "powerful leader"—implying women should be more passive and let men take charge.
- **A sexual orientation microaggression** could be a gay colleague being told not to flaunt their sexuality—the implicit message being that being gay is offensive and should be hidden.
- **A disability microaggression** could be when someone raises their voice when speaking to a blind person, despite the fact that the blind person's hearing is not impaired. This implies that their disability makes them inferior in all aspects of physical and mental functioning.
- **A class microaggression** could be constantly telling a colleague that their accent is difficult to understand—the hidden message being that they aren't part of affluent society and, therefore, are less than.

Equally, microaggressions occur when sweeping statements are made against everyone from the majority group, implying that they are part of the problem. For example, blaming all men for gender inequality or all White people for racism. These seemingly subtle interactions can have a significant psychological impact, leading to feelings of exclusion, anger, or frustration, and affecting the self-esteem of those being marginalized.

These subtle expressions of discrimination are pervasive because the majority of people consider themselves to be decent human beings and thus refuse to accept the reality that they hold biased views about others. The reality is that we all have a biased view of the world and, therefore, may say or do things that unintentionally make others feel oppressed or discriminated against. One of the prominent tools for assessing your unconscious bias is the Harvard Implicit Association Test,[46] which can be found online.

11

HOW TO SUSTAIN AND GROW HUMAN SKILLS

It's often said that a journey of a thousand miles begins with a single step. and this book represents that crucial first step toward self-discovery and personal growth. It empowers us to better understand ourselves and build deeper connections with those around us. Drawing on the profound philosophy of *Ubuntu*, the book illuminates the path to unleashing our collective human potential by honoring each other's humanity. As we embark on this transformative journey, the book emphasizes the importance of awareness, starting with cultivating self-awareness as we explore our values, dreams, passions, and beliefs. After all, we cannot truly understand others if we do not first understand ourselves. This journey also invites us to expand our awareness of others and embrace our emotions courageously, recognizing them as essential aspects of the inner strength we all possess.

This book paves the way for modern fulfillment by empowering us to embrace our role in cultivating a more connected and compassionate future. Growing up in rural Africa, I could not have envisioned that my journey would lead to this moment. What I did know, however, was that something powerful was embedded in the spirit of community that defined my village, where we understood the value of connection—and thrived because of it. In communities throughout Africa, the timeless wisdom of *Ubuntu* is cherished and passed down through generations, reminding us, "I am because we are." This profound truth rooted in our heritage empowers us to express our authentic selves and embrace the richness of our shared humanity. It has profoundly influenced my perspective on my role in the world and, importantly, how I choose to contribute. With this book, I pass forward the wisdom of my ancestors to you, with the hope that the enduring principles of *Ubuntu* will inspire transformative change in your life, just as they have indelibly transformed mine.

We live in an era defined by technology, social media, and an insatiable quest for more—more success, more possessions, and more recognition. This constant pursuit of external validation often distracts us from discovering what truly brings us joy and meaning. As a result, many of us struggle to attain real fulfillment in our lives. We end up feeling empty, disconnected, and overwhelmed by the pressure to keep up.

The book powerfully reminds us that genuine fulfillment doesn't come from the relentless pursuit of more, but from a deep understanding of ourselves and the vital connections we forge with others. It emphasizes our inherent human longing for connection, acceptance, and belonging, highlighting that true fulfillment cannot be realized in isolation. By highlighting our shared humanity—our *Ubuntu*—the book reveals how embracing the experiences of others and confronting our biases can cultivate meaningful relationships, making everyone feel valued and understood. It also offers the invaluable human skills to turn this understanding into action, paving the way for a richer and more purposeful life.

The book also serves as an essential guide for navigating the intricate challenges of today's workplaces and addressing the polarization in our society. These complexities often silence many individuals, preventing them from expressing their concerns on important issues.

By leveraging the power of human skills, this book empowers us to articulate our needs, make informed decisions, reduce difficulties at work, manage differences effectively, and flourish in diverse settings. It underscores that mastering these human skills is crucial for advancing our careers, fostering constructive relationships with supervisors, colleagues, and clients, and creating more inclusive workplaces. The book reveals how these skills can enhance the performance of diverse teams, making them more harmonious, innovative, and productive, ultimately driving significant business success. However, it also cautions that without equipping teams with these essential skills, organizations risk ongoing conflict and declining productivity.

As we continue to master our human skills, the practical strategies outlined in Parts II and III apply not only for the workplace, but for navigating everyday challenges and social interactions in our personal lives. These strategies shed light on how seemingly harmless phrases such as "I don't see color" can negatively impact people of color. They also emphasize the importance of setting healthy boundaries when dealing with an abusive partner, asserting that saying "no" is a complete sentence. They guide us in welcoming new immigrant families into our neighborhood, emphasizing that our role is to provide the kind of support they desire rather than attempting to "save" them.

With these invaluable strategies, we can fearlessly advocate for ourselves in various social situations. We can speak up at the next PTA meeting, understanding that our silence can be misconstrued as agreement. We can have respectful conversations with the young Gen Z barista at our neighborhood coffee shop, recognizing that despite their youthful exuberance, they can teach valuable lessons on prioritizing mental well-being. We can gracefully navigate prejudiced remarks from well-intentioned yet out-of-touch relatives. We can rebuild trust after experiencing a devastating betrayal from a close friend or loved one, knowing that forgiveness is just as much about freeing ourselves from pain and suffering as forgiving others.

HUMAN SKILLS

Now that we've found the courage to speak up, we have a new responsibility to use our voices to advocate for issues close to our hearts, fight against injustices, and bravely challenge the status quo and those who attempt to silence us. Consistently using our voices is the most effective way to prevent us from relapsing into silence.

Lastly, we must continuously enhance our human skills and remain curious to live more fulfilling lives. Learning should be a lifelong journey, as should the quest for greater self-awareness, emotional awareness, and social awareness. Our personal qualities constantly evolve, shaped by every experience, setback, and achievement. Thus, it's crucial to be attuned to these changes and actively process them to continue growing.

As you continue to learn and evolve, consider focusing on one area for improvement. Can you practice more patience with your loved ones, show greater empathy towards others, or view yourself with more compassion and less judgment? Now that you're more self-aware, it would be a huge loss not to work towards self-improvement or underestimate your ability to change for the better. Embracing negative self-perceptions and resigning to undesired behaviors only perpetuates dissatisfaction. Thus, start taking proactive steps toward positive change today.

On a final note of encouragement, I share this timeless tale from Aesop's Fables.[47] This story about a farmer and his donkey, passed down to me by my grandmother, Gogo, emphasizes the importance of knowing ourselves when navigating life.

One scorching afternoon, an old farmer and his young son embarked on a journey to the market to purchase sacks of seed for the upcoming planting season. They took their trusty donkey along to ease the burden of carrying the heavy load. As they made their way up a hill, leaving their farm behind, they encountered a group of young men lounging under a tree.

"Hey, farmer," one of the young men shouted, "what's the point of a donkey if you don't ride it?"

Embarrassed, the farmer lifted his son onto the donkey's back, and they resumed their journey. As they continued, the farmer and his son encountered a shepherd tending to his goats in the nearby pastures.

"What has the world come to," the shepherd remarked, "when a young boy lets his elderly father suffer while he rides?"

Feeling ashamed, the farmer commanded his son to dismount the donkey and took his place. Not long after, they encountered two women returning from the market.

"Oh, poor child," the farmer overheard one of the women bemoan. "What kind of a heartless man lets his son trudge along in this heat?"

Now, the farmer was confused. *What to do?* he pondered. He lifted his son onto the donkey in front of him, and they continued. As they approached the market, a jeering mob ran toward them, pointing and mocking.

"Look at you!" an angry heckler screamed at the farmer. "Have you no shame, overburdening that poor donkey with the weight of both of you?!"

Feeling the impact of the heckler's words, the farmer and his son dismounted the donkey. Next to them were two large branches from a tree. *I know what to do*, the farmer thought to himself. With determination, he tied the donkey across them. Drenched in sweat with the sun beating down on them, the farmer and his son lifted the donkey onto their shoulders. The mob erupted with laughter.

The farmer's attempt to please everyone failed to please anyone, including himself. The story reminds us that attempting to satisfy everyone will ultimately lead to dissatisfaction for ourselves and others. Without self-awareness, we can easily lose our way; but by mastering our human skills, we can avoid the farmer's fate.

ACKNOWLEDGMENTS

I'm grateful to Suzan Bymel, Emily Rapp Black, Ryan D. Herbage, Brendan Dunphy, Shannon Dunphy, Alison Rowe, and Presley Pizzo for their invaluable contributions to various aspects of this work and for helping define the book's vision.

Special thanks to my many collaborators who courageously broke their silence and shared their stories and struggles with me. Your perspectives deepened my understanding of workplace cultures and made this book possible.

To my creative partner, Jay Dawson, thank you for your inspiring ideas and passion, which always fuel my creativity and make our collaboration incredibly impactful.

To my editors, Jocelyn Carbonara, Andrew Dawson, and Conni Francini, thank you for your perspectives, feedback, and encouragement.

I am deeply grateful to Nan Graham and Sally Howe at Scribner for believing in me with my debut book. Their faith ignited my passion and convinced me that I could truly be a writer.

To my family, friends, and the African community, your unwavering support and unconditional love remind me every day that 'I am because we are.' Thank you for being my foundation.

Finally, to the incredible readers who supported my first book, *I Am a Girl from Africa*, I hope you enjoy reading this book as much as I enjoyed writing it. Your support has been a constant source of inspiration, and I am deeply grateful for it. Thank you.

RECOMMENDED READING

This brief list barely scratches the surface of the abundance of excellent resources waiting for those ready to take the initiative to seek them out; it serves as a mere starting point.

BOOKS

Brooks, David. 2023. How to Know a Person: The Art of Seeing Others Deeply and Being Deeply Seen. New York: Random House.

DiAngelo, Robin. 2018. White Fragility: Why It's So Hard for White People to Talk About Racism. Boston: Beacon Press.

Duhigg, Charles. 2018. Supercommunicators: How to Unlock the Secret Language of Connection. New York: Random House.

Grant, Adam. 2021. Think Again: The Power of Knowing What You Don't Know. New York: Viking.

Klaus, Peggy. 2007. The Hard Truth About Soft Skills: Workplace Lessons Smart People Wish They'd Learned Sooner. New York: Harper Collins.

Lordan, Grace. 2021. Think Big: Take Small Steps and Build the Future You Want.

Reiner, Andrew. 2020. Better Boys, Better Men: The New Masculinity That Creates Greater Courage and Emotional Resiliency. New York: Harper One.

Sinek, Simon. 2009. Start with Why: How Great Leaders Inspire Everyone to Take Action. Portfolio/Penguin.

ARTICLES

Bhambra, Manmit. "How Do We Bring More Diverse Voices into the Conversation about Inclusion?" Https://Www.Lse.Ac.Uk/

Research/Research-for-the-world/Race-equity/How-do-we-bring-more-diverse-voices-into-the-conversation-about-inclusion. London School of Economics and Political Science, November 9, 2021.

Read, Simon. "Employers in the US Are Cutting Back on Paternity Leave." World Economic Forum. October 3, 2022.

Nugent, Julie S., Alixandra Pollack, and Dnika J. Travis. *The Day-to-Day Experiences of Workplace Inclusion and Exclusion*. New York: Catalyst, 2016.

O.C. Tanner. *Global Culture Report*. 2024, "The Guide to Allyship." The Guide to Allyship, 2016. https://guidetoallyship.com/.

Walker, Bryan, and Sarah A. Soule. "Changing Company Culture Requires a Movement, Not a Mandate." *Harvard Business Review*, June 20, 2017.

FILMS

Demetrakas, Johanna, director. *Feminists: What Were They Thinking?* Netflix, 2018.

DuVernay, Ava, director. *13TH*. Netflix, 2016.

Siebel Newsom, Jennifer, director. *The Mask You Live In*. The Representation Project, 2015.

NOTES

INTRODUCTION
1. Biko, Steve. 1978. I Write What I Like. Heinemann.

CHAPTER 1
2. Oishi, Shigehiro and Ed Diener. "Residents of Poor Nations Have a Greater Sense of Meaning in Life Than Residents of Wealthy Nations." *Sage Journals*, (2013). Accessed January 25, 2024. https://doi.org/10.1177/0956797613507286.
3. "How Centering Purpose in the Workplace Fosters Empowerment." McKinsey & Company. August 25, 2024. https://www.mckinsey.com/featured-insights/mckinsey-guide-to-getting-unstuck/how-centering-purpose-in-the-workplace-fosters-empowerment.
4. Dixon-Fyle, Sundiatu, Celia Huber, María del Mar Martínez Márquez, and Sara Prince. "Diversity Matters Even More: The Case for Holistic Impact." Https://Www.Mckinsey.Com/Featured-insights/Diversity-and-inclusion/Diversity-matters-even-more-the-case-for-holistic-impact. McKinsey, December 5, 2023.
5. Frei, Frances X. and Anne Morriss. "Begin with Trust: The First Step to Becoming a Genuinely Empowering Leader." *Harvard Business Review*, January, 2017.
6. Ashok, Tupakula Dr. "The Significance of Soft Skills: an Overview." *International Journal of Academic Research 1*, no. 3 (2014). Accessed March 18, 2023. http://www.ijar.org.in/stuff/issues/sep-14/V-1-I-3-sep14.pdf
7. World Economic Forum (May 1, 2023). "Future of jobs 2023: These are the most in-demand skills now - and beyond." Retrieved July 19, 2023, from https://www.weforum.org/agenda/2023/05/future-of-jobs-2023-skills/
8. Berger, Guy Ph.D. "Data Reveals The Most In-Demand Soft Skills Among Candidates." https://www.linkedin.com/business/talent/blog/talent-strategy/most-indemand-soft-skills. LinkedIn, August 30, 2016.

CHAPTER 2

9   Tzu, Sun. 2006. *The Art of War*. Filiquarian Publishing, LLC.
10   "Douglas Adams on David Letterman." (February 14, 1985). DJ Solid Snail. June 9, 2012. https://www.youtube.com/watch?v=SF2fZ2iOXhk.
11   Eurich, Tasha. "Working with People Who Aren't Self-Aware." *Harvard Business Review*, October 19, 2018.
12   Duhigg, Charles. 2018. Supercommunicators: How to Unlock the Secret Language of Connection. New York: Random House.
13   Bradberry, Travis Dr, and Dr. Jean Greaves. 2009. *Emotional Intelligence 2.0*. San Diego: TalentSmart.
14   Landry, Lauren. "Why Emotional Intelligence Is Important in Leadership." Harvard Business School. April 3, 2019. https://online.hbs.edu/blog/post/emotional-intelligence-in-leadership.

CHAPTER 3

15   Brodnitz, Dan. "The Most In-Demand Skills for 2024." LinkedIn. February 8, 2024. https://www.linkedin.com/business/talent/blog/talent-strategy/linkedin-most-in-demand-hard-and-soft-skills.
16   "Maya Angelou Quotable Quote." Goodreads. https://www.goodreads.com/quotes/5934-i-ve-learned-that-people-will-forget-what-you-said-people.
17   Djurovic, Ana. "Remote Working Statistics to Get You Going - 2023 Edition." Goremotely, March 7, 2023. https://goremotely.net/blog/remote-working-statistics.
18   Stevenson, Alexandra. "A Push for Gender Equality at the Davos World Economic Forum and Beyond." *New York Times* (New York), January 19, 2016.

CHAPTER 4

19   "2022 Edelman Trust Barometer." Edelman. January 18, 2022.
20   Zak, Paul J. "The Neuroscience of Trust." *Harvard Business Review*, January 1, 2017.
21   Frei, Frances X. and Anne Morriss. "Begin with Trust: The First Step to Becoming a Genuinely Empowering Leader." *Harvard Business Review*, May, 2020.
22   "Uncovering Culture: A Call to Action for Leaders." Deloitte. 2024. https://www2.deloitte.com/us/en/pages/about-deloitte/articles/uncovering-culture.html.
23   Frei, Frances X. and Anne Morriss. "Begin with Trust: The First Step to Becoming a Genuinely Empowering Leader." *Harvard Business Review*, May, 2020.

CHAPTER 5

24 "American Psychiatric Association's (APA) Annual Mental Health Poll, 2024." The American Institute of Stress, July 5, 2024.
25 "Guidelines on Mental Health at Work." World Health Organization. September 28, 2022. https://www.who.int/publications/i/item/9789240053052

CHAPTER 6

26 Mehrabian, Albert. 1981. Silent Messages: Implicit Communication of Emotions and Attitudes. Wadsworth Pub. Co.
27 Donelly, B. (June 15, 2016). "Male chief executives with daughters more likely to champion gender diversity." The Sydney Morning Herald.
28 Amar, A. D., C. Hentrich, & V. Hlupic. (December 2009). To Be a Better Leader, Give Up Authority. Harvard Business Review.
29 "Mind the Gap." KPMG, 2022. https://assets.kpmg.com/content/dam/kpmg/xx/pdf/2022/12/mind-the-gap.pdf

CHAPTER 7

30 DiAngelo, Robin. 2018. White Fragility: Why It's So Hard for White People to Talk About Racism. Boston: Beacon Press.
31 Ibid

CHAPTER 8

32 "Harnessing the Power of a Multigenerational Workforce." SHRM Foundation. The Society of Human Resource Management, October 2, 2017. https://www.shrm.org/content/dam/en/shrm/foundation/2017%20TL%20Executive%20Summary-FINAL.pdf.
33 Urick, Michael J., Elaine C. Hollensbe, Suzanne S. Masterson, and Sean T. Lyons. "Understanding and Managing Intergenerational Conflict: An Examination of Influences and Strategies." *Oxford Academia*, (2017). Accessed March 21, 2024.
34 Brooks, David. 2023. How to Know a Person: The Art of Seeing Others Deeply and Being Deeply Seen. New York: Random House.
35 De Smet, Aaron, Marino Mugayar-Baldocchi, Angelika Reich, and Bill Schaninger. "Gen What? Debunking Age-based Myths about Worker Preferences." McKinsey. April 20, 2023. https://www.mckinsey.com/capabilities/people-and-organizational-performance/our-insights/gen-what-debunking-age-based-myths-about-worker-preferences.
36 Pettigrew, Thomas Fraser. "Intergroup Contact Theory." *PubMed*, (1998). https://doi.org/10.1146/annurev.psych.49.1.65.

37 "Enhancing Intergenerational Communication, Bridging the Gap in Global and Dispersed Teams." Berkeley ExeEdu. https://executive.berkeley.edu/thought-leadership/blog/enhancing-intergenerational-communication.

38 "2024 Gen Z and Millennial Survey: Living and Working with Purpose in a Transforming World." Deloitte, May 15, 2024. https://www.deloitte.com/global/en/issues/work/content/genz-millennialsurvey.html.

CHAPTER 9

39 "Adam Grant, X Social Media Post." Https://X.Com/AdamMGrant. June 18, 2022. Video, https://x.com/AdamMGrant/status/1538158767426179072?lang=en.

40 "Uncovering Culture: A Call to Action for Leaders." Deloitte, November 14, 2023. https://www2.deloitte.com/us/en/pages/about-deloitte/articles/uncovering-culture.html

CHAPTER 10

41 "Allyship for Gender Equity at Work." John Hopkins Carey Business School. January 18, 2024.

42 Hideg, Ivona , Anya Krstic, Raymond Trau, and Tanya Zarina. "Do Longer Maternity Leaves Hurt Women's Careers?" *Harvard Business Review*, September 14, 2018. https://hbr.org/2018/09/do-longer-maternity-leaves-hurt-womens-careers.

43 Kochhar, Rakesh. "The Enduring Grip of the Gender Pay Gap." Pew Research Center, March 1, 2023. https://executive.berkeley.edu/thought-leadership/blog/enhancing-intergenerational-communication.

44 Schneider, Monica E., Brenda Major, Riia Luhtanen, and Jennifer Crocker. "Social Stigma and the Potential Costs of Assumptive Help." *Sage Journals*, (1996). Accessed November 11, 2023. https://journals.sagepub.com/doi/abs/10.1177/0146167296222009

45 Pizzo, Presley. "The 'Boots and Sandals' Exercise." Parts with Presley. https://partswithpresley.com/about/.

46 "Harvard Implicit Association Test." Harvard, 2011. https://implicit.harvard.edu/implicit/takeatest.html.

CHAPTER 11

47 "The Miller, His Son, & the Ass." Library of Congress Aesop Fables. https://read.gov/aesop/136.html.